FATAL FEVER

TRACKING DOWN TYPHOID MARY

Gail Jarrow

CALKINS CREEK
AN IMPRINT OF HIGHLIGHTS
Honesdale, Pennsylvania

For information about permission to reproduce selections from this book, please contact permissions@highlights.com.

Calkins Creek
An Imprint of Highlights
815 Church Street
Honesdale, Pennsylvania 18431
Printed in China

ISBN: 978-1-62091-597-4

Library of Congress Control Number: 2014948476

First edition

10 9 8 7 6 5 4 3 2 1

Production by Margaret Mosomillo
Titles set in Helvetica Neue LT Std 107 Extra Black Condensed Oblique
Text set in Eames Century Modern

Half title: Typhoid fever is caused by *Salmonella* Typhi, a rod-shaped bacterium that uses whiplike flagella to move.

Title page: An 1882 painting of a typhoid patient shows her bloody nose and spots on her skin, symptoms of the disease.

Contents

For Tate, who knows a thing or two about sleuthing

Acknowledgments

Thanks to those who helped me research, write, and polish this book:

Dr. Eric Mintz, lead for the Centers for Disease Control and Prevention's Global Water, Sanitation, and Hygiene Epidemiology Team, for graciously sharing his expertise, sending me relevant scientific papers, and checking the accuracy of the typhoid information in my manuscript.

Dr. Judith Walzer Leavitt, professor emerita, Department of Medical History and Bioethics, University of Wisconsin–Madison, who took the time to answer my lingering questions about Mary Mallon.

Dr. Mark McKinlay, director of the Center for Vaccine Equity, the Task Force for Global Health, for his assistance in getting answers to my technical questions.

Susan Soper, who helped me piece together details about the life of her great-grandfather George A. Soper.

Peter Dabback, science teacher in the Spring-Ford Area School District, Royersford, Pennsylvania, who connected me with typhoid fever experts.

The staffs at the Division of Rare and Manuscript Collections, Cornell University Library; the Newspaper & Current Periodical Reading Room, Library of Congress; and the Microforms Reading Room, Schwarzman Building, New York Public Library.

The entire team at Calkins Creek, who brought my manuscript to print. I'm particularly grateful to Joan Hyman for her eagle eye. Special thanks go to Carolyn P. Yoder, my incomparable editor, for once again accompanying me on a journey into history.

Finally, I appreciate the support of my patient and tolerant husband, Robert Jarrow. He never once complained about my unappetizing typhoid fever dinner conversations.

—GJ

1

HIDDEN

"I am an innocent human being." —Mary Mallon

Early on a damp March morning in 1907, Mary Mallon answered the knock at the servants' entrance of a New York brownstone house. She took one look at the visitors and lunged at them with her sharp fork. As they flinched, she ran toward the kitchen.

Mary knew why they were there. A few weeks earlier, a well-dressed man with a mustache had shown up, accusing her of outrageous and horrible things. Later, he followed her. Cornered her at her friend's home. Acted as though he had the right to stick her with a needle and steal her blood.

Yesterday, a woman in a tailored suit and stiff collar had come to the kitchen. She claimed to have the authority to do exactly that . . . and more. The woman refused to take Mary's "no" for an answer. Now she was back with the police.

Mary was sure that this time, if they caught her, they

wouldn't let her go. She should have disappeared when she had the chance. They had no right to threaten her or touch her body. Even if she was only a cook, Mary wasn't going to let them do it.

Picking up her skirts, she fled past the kitchen and down the hall.

Where could she hide? Mary headed for the back door. Frantically, she scanned the snow-covered yard for a hiding place, but she saw nothing. Policemen were looking for her inside the house and out on the street. She was trapped.

A high wooden fence separated the backyard from the house next door. If she could just get over that fence and into the neighbor's yard . . .

A wooden chair pushed up against the fence would do the trick.

Thank Almighty God she had friends who would help. Would say that they had no idea where she'd gone. Would point out a small outside closet under the neighbor's front steps. Would pile some ash cans against its closed door after she climbed in.

Mary shut the door behind her and crouched down.

She didn't know it, but she wasn't alone in that cramped, cold closet. Deep inside her body, billions of deadly microorganisms were hiding, too.

The fates of three people collided at that New York City brownstone. The three had been born within four years of each other and had taken different paths to reach the middle of their lives. In late winter 1907, those lives changed forever.

For George Albert Soper, determined to establish his reputation, the event would add another triumph to boost his career.

For Sara Josephine Baker, attempting to make her mark in a male-dominated and often corrupt city government, it would bolster her efforts to gain respect and responsibility.

For Mary Mallon, struggling to support herself in an adopted country, her encounters with both of them would lead to a notoriety that has lasted for more than a century. The world would remember who she was long after it had forgotten the other two.

These three people were brought together by a dreaded scourge that left behind shattered dreams, broken hearts, and painful death.

TYPHOID FEVER.

2

GERM DETECTIVE

"One very disagreeable fact about typhoid fever is that it is intimately associated with human excrements." —William Sedgwick

Deadly diseases had affected George Soper's life from its beginning in 1870. Two months before George was born in Brooklyn, New York, his father died of tuberculosis, leaving a pregnant widow and two-year-old daughter.

When George was twelve, the German scientist Robert Koch announced his discovery of the tuberculosis bacterium, the microbe that had killed Mr. Soper and millions more. The medical community began to understand that other diseases, including typhoid fever, were also caused by germs that could be transmitted between people.

Lethal microbes had plenty of opportunity to spread as the population of the United States exploded. By the time George Soper turned thirty, he had seen the nation's size double to 76 million as immigrants flooded in. Many of the newcomers settled in the fast-growing cities. In 1870, only

25 percent of the American population lived in urban areas. By 1900, that number had increased to 40 percent.

Crowded cities, like New York where George grew up, were grimy, stinking, unsanitary places. Raw sewage fouled the water. Mountains of spoiled food and garbage lined the sidewalks, rotting in the sun. Horses dropped 2,000 tons of manure on streets every day. The city was littered with dead and decomposing animals, including cattle, donkeys, dogs, rats, and more than 10,000 horses a year. Too many people lived crammed together in filthy, poorly built tenement buildings that had overflowing outhouses.

This environment was hard on the body. A white male born in a major American city was likely to die ten years sooner than one born in a rural area.

GERM FIGHTING

Doctors, scientists, and public health officials realized that by controlling or eliminating germs, they could prevent some of the deadly diseases. Engineers went to work designing ways to improve dirty living conditions.

George Soper wanted to be part of the sanitation movement, and a career in engineering was a way to do that. He studied for his bachelor's degree in engineering at Rensselaer Polytechnic Institute in Troy, New York, located along the Hudson River north of New York City.

As a student, George joined the battle against infectious diseases. While spending one Christmas vacation in New York State's Adirondack Mountains, he heard about two typhoid fever patients living nearby. Their rented house had a history of harboring typhoid and other contagious diseases. George decided that the building was too unsanitary to be safe, and he helped the two patients and their families move out. Then he convinced the house's

George Soper (1870–1948)

owner that the best way to deal with such a cursed place was to destroy it. With the owner's permission, George burned it down.

After Soper received his degree, he worked as a civil engineer for the Boston Waterworks and for a company that built systems to filter drinking water. Later, he returned to New York City and enrolled at Columbia University where, in 1899, he earned his Ph.D. in engineering.

Armed with this training, Soper set up a consulting business on Broadway in Lower Manhattan. He advertised himself as a "Sanitary Engineer and Chemist." Communities throughout the country hired him to study their sanitation systems, find the defects, and suggest ways to fix them. Soper became known as a "germ detective."

FECES, FINGERS, AND FLIES

It was Soper's business to know everything about typhoid fever—what caused it, how it spread, and how to stop it.

Typhoid was among the top five fatal infectious diseases in the United States, along with influenza, pneumonia, tuberculosis, and diphtheria. In 1900, it struck nearly 400,000 Americans, and more than 35,000 of them died.

Only humans catch typhoid fever. Only humans pass it to others. The typhoid bacterium doesn't need an intermediary host like a mosquito, which carries malaria and yellow fever from human to human when it bites them.

Instead, the germ travels from the feces and urine of one person to the mouth of another, usually by way of water or food. Under the right conditions, it can survive several weeks in water and soil.

George Soper had seen what happened when typhoid

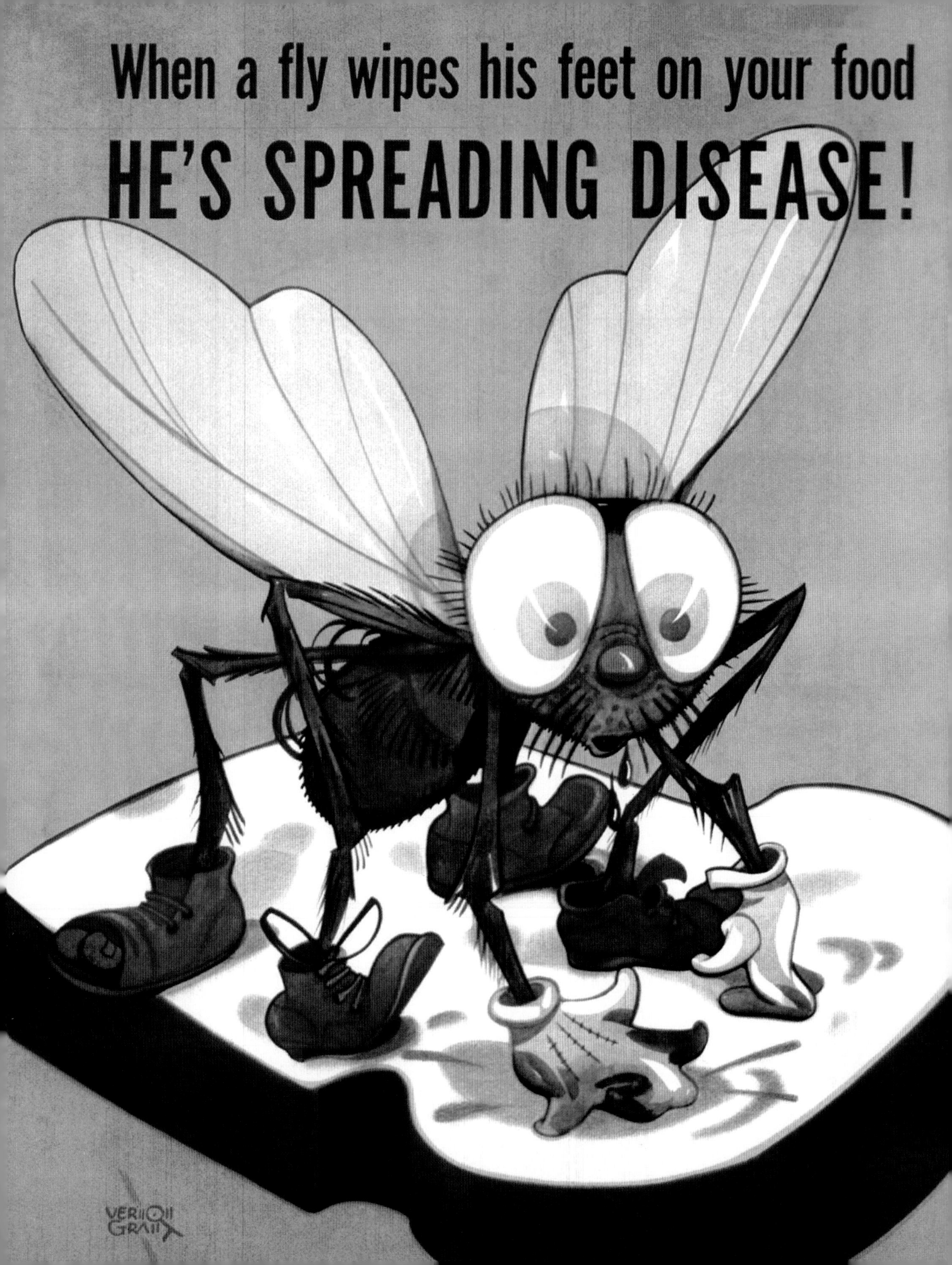
When a fly wipes his feet on your food
HE'S SPREADING DISEASE!

germs infected someone. The victim started to feel sick between one to three weeks after ingesting the bacteria. Maybe he drank river water contaminated with sewage from the town upstream. Or perhaps she ate a salad doused with well water polluted by oozing waste from an outhouse. Or he swallowed raw shellfish taken from a bay where sewage was dumped. Maybe it was the unpasteurized milk that had been poured into a milk pail recently rinsed out with bacteria-laden water.

Cooking killed typhoid germs, but food could still be contaminated before it was eaten. A person touched it with unwashed fingers carrying bits of feces. A fly landed, its legs transporting human waste from a recent visit to an unscreened outhouse. If food sat too long at room temperature, these bacteria multiplied, creating even more dangerous germs.

In the early twentieth century, doctors referred to typhoid as a disease caused by the four Fs: feces, food, fingers, and flies. Dr. William Sedgwick, a Massachusetts scientist and epidemiologist, observed: "Dirt, diarrhea and dinner too often get sadly confused."

GHASTLY SYMPTOMS

The typhoid victim probably had forgotten, or never knew, when he was infected with the bacteria. But now he had a headache, felt tired and weak, and had lost his appetite. As the disease progressed, his temperature rose as high as 104 degrees and he no longer had the energy to get out of bed. Other symptoms appeared, including abdominal pain, constipation, chills, and red spots on the chest and abdomen.

The illness typically lasted three to four weeks. Some people had mild cases with few symptoms,

Opposite: A U.S. government poster warns about germ-carrying flies.

Bottom: William Sedgwick (1855–1921), a biology professor at the Massachusetts Institute of Technology, influenced the public health field through his teaching and studies of typhoid epidemics.

How typhoid bacteria spread: sewage leaks into a well from an outhouse and from a stream where women dump chamber pots.

barely realizing they were sick. Others struggled for months to recover. In the most severe cases, patients became delirious, developed diarrhea, and bled profusely from the intestines. They grew weaker until they died, often in agonizing pain.

For about 10 to 30 percent of typhoid patients, the disease was fatal. No one was sure why people reacted so differently. Doctors guessed that it depended on the amount of bacteria victims ingested, the strength of their

immune systems, and the quality of the nursing care they received.

In the early 1900s, the basic treatment was to keep patients comfortable in bed, using sponge baths to lower body temperature. No medicine or tonic would kill the bacteria as they multiplied and damaged the body. No surgical procedure could remove the microorganisms. Typhoid fever had to run its course until the victim's immune system defeated it or he died. Those who survived usually were protected from future attacks.

KEEP OUT THE SEWAGE

George Soper was aware that the "discharges from a single patient [had] been known to pollute the entire water supply of a city sufficiently to cause a serious epidemic of typhoid fever." All it took to infect someone was "less than one glass of water containing typhoid bacilli."

The way to protect the public was to stop sewage from entering water sources—streams, rivers, lakes, and wells—and to purify contaminated drinking water. Engineers like Soper were confident that if those changes happened, typhoid epidemics would end. London, Paris, and Berlin had already seen far fewer outbreaks as a result of their efforts to keep water supplies free of sewage.

The United States lagged behind Europe, but it was improving. During Soper's childhood in the early 1880s, nearly 1 in 5 Americans could expect to get typhoid during his or her lifetime. By the beginning of the twentieth century, better sanitation had brought that rate down to about 1 in 10.

Still, in 1900, thousands of New York City's 3.5 million residents caught the disease. More than 700 died, a typhoid death rate almost four times that of Berlin, Germany.

In the city of Troy, New York, where Soper had gone to college, typhoid's fatality rate during the same year was seven times higher than New York City's. In one outbreak, hundreds of Troy's 60,000 inhabitants were infected, and 93 died.

Towns and rural areas, where the majority of Americans lived in 1900, didn't escape. Typhoid broke out when waste from outhouses leaked into wells and surface water. The press paid less attention to these epidemics because fewer people became ill than in a large city. Yet the impact on a community was devastating.

During the winter of 1903, typhoid fever invaded Ithaca, New York, two hundred miles northwest of New York City. The disease spread among not only the 13,000 townspeople but also the 3,000 Cornell University students. As the epidemic grew, so did fear and panic.

Germ detective George Soper would find himself at the center of this frightening outbreak.

Typhoid Fever

Typhoid fever has plagued humans since prehistoric times. Genetic research suggests that the bacteria might have been around for twenty thousand years, even before humans settled into villages and developed agriculture.

Typhoid wasn't recognized as a separate disease until the late 1830s. Before that, doctors confused it with typhus, which is caused by a microbe spread by lice, fleas, mites, and ticks. Typhoid got its name because its symptoms—high fever and rash—resembled those of typhus. Both names come from the Greek word for *foggy* or *hazy*, which refers to a feverish patient's mental condition.

Doctors once thought that typhoid fever, like many diseases, was caused by a miasma, air poisoned by decaying

Early in the twentieth century, most people believed that dust spread contagious diseases. In this 1900 *Puck* magazine cartoon, a servant sweeps a carpet, releasing deadly clouds of typhoid fever, consumption (tuberculosis), influenza, germs, and microbes.

organic material. This idea seemed reasonable since sicknesses were often linked to smelly sewer gases, swampy ground, stagnant water, and decomposing animals and plants.

Then during the 1840s, British physician William Budd (1811–1880) began a study of typhoid fever after he almost died of it. He discovered a connection between the outbreak of new cases and water contaminated with the feces of typhoid patients. In 1856, Budd advised fellow physicians that the disease's spread could be prevented by boiling drinking water and by chemically disinfecting typhoid patients' excrement and soiled linens.

No one realized then that microorganisms caused diseases. This idea, called the germ theory, took hold in the medical community during the 1880s and 1890s, thanks to research by Louis Pasteur (1822–1895), Robert Koch (1843–1910), and others. In 1880, Karl Eberth (1835–1926), a German microbiologist, identified a bacterium found in typhoid patients as the microbe behind the disease. Today it is known as *Salmonella* Typhi. The bacterium is related to other types of *Salmonella* that cause food poisoning symptoms such as diarrhea and vomiting. But their effects are milder than *Salmonella* Typhi's and usually not fatal.

A typhoid fever victim can give off a trillion of the bacteria in each gram of his or her feces (about the weight of a paper clip). A small fraction of that is enough to produce infection in someone who swallows them.

The bacteria travel to this person's stomach, where

acid kills some. The rest enter the small intestine, where they invade the intestinal lining and cross into the bloodstream.

As these bacteria multiply and spread, they may cause infections throughout the body, including in the liver, gallbladder, spleen, bone marrow, lungs, heart, and kidneys. The bacteria do their deadliest damage in the intestines.

Dr. William Budd's 1859 photograph shows the holes caused by deadly typhoid bacteria in a victim's small intestine.

They may trigger profuse bleeding or create holes that allow the contents of the intestine to escape into the abdominal cavity. This can lead to a slow, painful death and is the major cause of typhoid fatalities.

Typhoid fever's early symptoms resemble other illnesses, making it hard to diagnose. In 1903, it was often confused with influenza, called grippe. At that time, the preferred—though not foolproof—way to confirm typhoid was the Widal blood test.

Developed in 1896 by French physician Georges Widal (1862–1929), the method uses a few drops of the patient's blood mixed with a specially grown culture of typhoid bacteria. If the person has typhoid fever, his blood contains antibodies against the bacteria. These antibodies react with the bacteria in the culture, causing them to clump. The Widal test isn't accurate until the patient has been sick for several days and has built up sufficient antibodies.

In the early 1900s, urine was tested, too, using a chemical mixture that changed color if the patient had typhoid. In another test, a sample of feces was cultured. The bacteria that grew were examined through a microscope to see if they were *Salmonella* Typhi.

Today the Widal test is no longer considered dependable enough to diagnose typhoid fever. But it is still used, particularly in developing countries, because it's simple to do and gives fast results. The most reliable diagnostic method is to culture a sample of bone marrow, although obtaining the sample is an invasive procedure that can be painful. Instead, cultures of blood, feces, and urine are more commonly used to confirm the presence of typhoid bacteria.

DEATH IN ITHACA

"The death is particularly sad inasmuch as neither of the deceased's relatives was able to be at the boy's bedside." —Ithaca Daily News

The first hint of trouble came on January 11, 1903, when a feverish Ithacan sought a doctor's help. Within days, people all over town collapsed into their beds, too weak to move. Soon more than a dozen patients a day were admitted to the city hospital and to Cornell University's infirmary.

Doctors initially thought they were dealing with an intestinal flu. On January 21, a local newspaper reported 96 cases of grippe. That was wishful thinking. As the symptoms progressed, it became clear that a disease far more dangerous had come to Ithaca—typhoid fever.

One of the city's newspapers began publishing the names of the sick and the dead. The first to die was William Spence, age forty-eight, who lost his battle with typhoid on January 23.

Oliver Shumard was among the Cornell students who fell ill. The son of a Missouri farmer, he had entered the university the previous fall on a scholarship to study philosophy. On January 25, Oliver was admitted to the student infirmary with early symptoms of typhoid.

After three days, he was no better. As other student patients gradually improved, Oliver's condition worsened, and Cornell officials notified his family. Filled with dread, Oliver's father immediately boarded a train from Missouri, hoping his son would still be alive when he got to Ithaca.

Just about everyone had a friend or a neighbor or an acquaintance who was suffering with typhoid fever. It seemed as if a black cloud of disease covered the city. Where had it come from? And how could they get rid of it?

POISON WATER

Most of the sick had obtained their drinking water from the private company that supplied the city. Although Ithaca sat on forty-mile-long Cayuga Lake, the water was too polluted to drink. The city sewer system dumped raw human waste into an inlet of the lake. It produced "a scum of undigested sewage material, unsightly and malodorous, drifting with the wind and building up along the shore."

The company instead pumped the city's water from two local creeks. The stream water didn't look as polluted as the lake, but it often had a foul smell and taste. Like many American communities in the early 1900s, the company neither filtered the water to remove feces and other contaminants nor purified it with chemicals to kill bacteria.

Everyone soon realized that the typhoid victims' drinking water came from the same stream, Six Mile Creek.

As the typhoid epidemic spread, the *Ithaca Daily News* printed a warning to boil contaminated drinking water.

Boil the Water!

Health Officer Hitchcock requests the News to state that citizens should bear in mind that common filters do not purify drinking water, and that boiling is the only safe way to prevent contamination.

All are urged to boil the water for several minutes before using. This alone will kill the germs which are supposed to be causing the present epidemic.

Top: Cornell University's infirmary, housed in a mansion near the campus, soon became overcrowded with sick students.

Bottom: In February 1903, a newspaper cartoon captured the anguish of Ithacans as they nursed the typhoid victims, many of whom were young adults.

Two Cornell professors, in bacteriology and in chemistry, tested the creek's water. They found that it was contaminated with bacteria commonly found in human feces.

Typhoid bacteria were difficult to separate and identify from the other intestinal microbes in the polluted water. But because so many people developed typhoid fever after drinking from the creek, the professors concluded that typhoid bacteria *were* likely there. The public was drinking "death-dealing impurities."

On January 29, more than two weeks after the first cases appeared, the city's health officer told Ithacans to boil drinking water obtained from the water company. Terrified parents removed faucet handles so that their children couldn't turn on the water. The school superintendent hired a plumber to cut off city water to all schools, except for flushing toilets.

Cornell University cautioned its students in a written notice: "DO NOT RELAX CARE in regard to water used for brushing the teeth, or taken for any purpose into the mouth. Do not eat uncooked oysters. Do not take any cold drinks nor eat ice cream or uncooked food down town."

Unfortunately, these actions were too late to prevent the typhoid bacteria from attacking the bodies of those who had already swallowed them. As many as three weeks could pass before an infected person showed symptoms. New cases appeared every day after the boil order was issued.

By the beginning of February, more than 340 people had typhoid fever. Ithaca's three dozen doctors could barely keep up with their house calls. The city hospital was overcrowded. The Cornell infirmary was designed to handle 20 patients, but the nurses there were caring for nearly 60.

To deal with all the sick, the city and university recruited extra nurses from out of town. Cots were set up in a church, in a house near the infirmary, and in the medical-college building on campus.

YOUNG VICTIMS

The outbreak seemed to hit the Cornell students the hardest, a fact that didn't surprise local doctors. Three years earlier, the federal census revealed that more than a third of typhoid victims were between the ages of fifteen and thirty.

No one was sure why. One hypothesis was that when people left their childhood homes and moved to new places, they were exposed to the bacteria for the first time. Although older Americans developed the disease, too, they did so less often. Perhaps an earlier typhoid bout had protected them.

On February 2, Oliver Shumard spent his twenty-sixth birthday in the Cornell infirmary. He was so deathly ill that he was unable to celebrate. Two days later, the infirmary nurses recorded that he was "very sick." Oliver's father arrived in Ithaca from Missouri in time to be by his son's bedside on Friday, February 6. Later that night, Oliver became the first Cornell student to die in the epidemic.

Sophomore Charlotte Spencer of Jasper, New York, was one of about four hundred women studying at Cornell. In 1903, few women had the opportunity to go to college. Charlotte's parents, who were farmers, were determined to educate all their six children, boys and girls.

When Charlotte was struck down by typhoid fever in late January, she was admitted to the Cornell infirmary.

This drawing of Charlotte Spencer appeared in a February 1903 newspaper article about the Ithaca typhoid epidemic.

By February 9, the typhoid bacteria had ravaged her body, and the young woman was failing.

"Much concern is felt regarding Miss C. E. Spencer, '05," reported an Ithaca newspaper. "She has grown steadily worse within the last 24 hours and the worst is expected."

Charlotte's mother rushed from Jasper seventy miles away to be at her side. During the early morning hours of February 10, the typhoid bacteria won out. Charlotte was the first and only female Cornell student to die.

Within a week, 7 fellow students joined Charlotte and Oliver in death. On a single day, February 17, 3 died.

One of them was Henry Schoenborn, a freshman from Hackensack, New Jersey, who had won a scholarship to study law. First in his high-school class, Henry was considered "a student of particular promise." When he entered the infirmary on January 31, he was already seriously ill. His worried mother traveled from New Jersey to do what she could for her son. But Henry's intestines began to hemorrhage. Once the bleeding started, nothing could save him.

Henry's grieving older brother William, a Cornell sophomore in mechanical engineering, quickly left Ithaca to escape the same fate. The next week he wrote Cornell's president, Jacob Schurman: "Hoping that the conditions at Ithaca may soon improve, so that my parents will permit me to return again to Cornell, I remain still a Cornellian."

CITY OF FEAR

The community was overwhelmed with sick and dying people. Local doctors sent home about 200 Cornell students when they first showed symptoms, believing the patients

CORNELL INFIRMARY.
(DAILY REPORT.)

190

NAME.	DATE OF ADMISSION.	DISEASE.	PHYSICIAN.	CONDITION OF PATIENT.
A. H. Schaaf	Jan 29	Typhoid	Orum	Improving.
J. W. Young	„ 31	Grippe	Beaman	„
H. A. Schoenborn	„ 31	Typhoid	„	very sick
Miss C. Spencer	„ 31	„	Cadie	„
W. A. Tydeman	Feb 1	„	Beaman	„
L. A. Kilburn	„ 1	„	„	Improving
S. H. Fringer	Jan 31	„	„	very sick
E. S. Choate	Feb 1	„	„	Improving.
G. A. Wessman	„ 1	„	Bigg	No improvement
W. Katzenstein	„ 1	Concussion of knee	Coville	Improving
E. S. Fletcher	„ 1	Paracolon fever	„	No improvement
B. G. Daboll	„ 1	Typhoid	Beaman	„
W. J. Wright	„ 2	Enteric fever	Wilson	Improving
J. H. McEvoy	„ 5	„	„	No improvement
A. P. Lord	„ 2	Paracolon fever	Coville	„
A. T. Freer	„ 2	Typhoid	Douglass	„
J. A. Woods	„ 3	„	„	„

Top (left to right): **Three Cornell students died on February 22: George Hill, William Reinhart, and Francis Swartz.** *Bottom:* **The Cornell Infirmary Daily Report lists five students who later died of typhoid fever: Henry Schoenborn, Charlotte Spencer, G. A. Wessman, J. H. McEvoy, and A. P. Lord.**

FEVER-STRICKEN ITHACA IS

would receive better nursing in their hometowns.

Hundreds of other students, afraid that they might be next, also left town, even though they wouldn't get credit for the classes they missed.

That didn't guarantee they would escape typhoid's death sentence. In late January, twenty-two-year-old agriculture student Charles Langworthy and his roommate, Edward Green, developed signs of typhoid. Their Ithaca doctor recommended that both young men take the one-hundred-mile train trip to their hometown of Alfred, New York. Glad to have them home, their families cared for them. But three weeks later, the typhoid bacteria attacked Charles's intestines, and he bled to death. Edward eventually recovered.

As the epidemic spread, newspapers across the country picked up the story and ran headlines about the "Scourge of Typhoid in Ithaca." Anxious parents of the students still at school sent frantic telegrams to President Schurman, asking whether their children were safe. He assured them that the university was providing clean water and instructions on avoiding infection.

Despite this, students continued to fall ill. Schurman received a daily update from the infirmary about each of its patients, and he telegraphed the report to parents. When the prognosis looked grim, he advised them to come to their child's bedside.

Some parents were angry that their children had been infected. One father, whose sophomore son returned home to New Jersey to recover, wrote: "I cannot but feel that the City authorities of Ithaca have been grossly negligent and careless regarding the water supply of the City, and I cannot escape from the feeling that the College authorities have not been blameless."

Jacob Schurman (1854–1942) served as Cornell's president from 1892 to 1920. This photograph appeared in the university's 1903 yearbook.

MOURNING FOR ITS DEAD.

The suffering and death would not stop. By Monday of the final week in February, 14 Cornell students and 16 townspeople had tragically succumbed. The dead included five-year-old Esther Howell, daughter of a city council member, and eleven-year-old Catherine Caveney, who lived a few blocks away from little Esther.

A New York City newspaper captured the town's emotions in a page-wide headline: "Fever-Stricken Ithaca Is In Mourning For Its Dead."

Form No. 102.

THE WESTERN UNION TELEGRAPH COMPANY
INCORPORATED
21,000 OFFICES IN AMERICA. CABLE SERVICE TO ALL THE WORLD.
THOS. T. ECKERT, President and General Manager.

Receiver's No.	Time Filed	Check

SEND the following message, subject to the terms on back hereof, which are hereby agreed to.

Feb. 12 1903

To H. E. Colvin,
423 Jackson St.,
Kansas City, Mo.

J. A. Woods sick with typhoid in Cornell Infirmary had severe hemorrhage last night. Condition critical.

J. G. S.

READ THE NOTICE AND AGREEMENT ON BACK.

Pres

C. W. J.

President Schurman sent many telegrams to students' families. J. A. Woods, who is listed at the bottom of the infirmary report on page 29, survived.

31

"AN ENEMY THAT MOVES IN THE DARK"

"Typhoid is one of the most difficult diseases to wholly extinguish in a place in which it has once gained a strong foothold." —George Soper

By the end of February, 1,000 students—more than a third of Cornell's student body—had fled the campus in fear for their lives. Some of them said they didn't intend to return to Ithaca and Cornell ever again. Major newspapers throughout the United States were regularly reporting on the outbreak. This wasn't the kind of publicity the university, city, or state wanted.

New York State Commissioner of Health Daniel Lewis was worried. Ithaca's leaders had struggled to get the epidemic under control. Lewis doubted that the local health department could handle the problem alone. Ithaca desperately needed expert help.

The commissioner contacted George Soper. Lewis had been impressed by the sanitary engineer's work in the fall of 1900, after a devastating hurricane killed more than 8,000 in Galveston, Texas. Soper had traveled there with a group to assist the Texans.

A house lies upended after a powerful hurricane struck Galveston, Texas, on September 8, 1900. It was the United States' deadliest natural disaster.

When he arrived in Galveston, Soper was shocked to find thousands of unburied bodies lying in the city's ruins. "It was nauseating in the extreme," he later said, "but it didn't produce typhoid fever." With typhoid, "there is more danger from the living than the dead."

He recommended ways to set up effective sanitation in Galveston while the community cleaned up from the destruction. His advice prevented disease outbreaks like typhoid among the hurricane's survivors.

Soper had rescued Galveston, and Commissioner Lewis wanted him to do the same for Ithaca. He asked the thirty-three-year-old to go there as a representative of the state health department.

George Soper felt confident that he could stop the outbreak's spread. He had experience handling exactly this kind of challenge. So on Tuesday, March 3, 1903, he said good-bye to his wife, Mary Virginia, and their two little boys, George and Harvey, and boarded a train from New York City headed to the heart of the epidemic.

NO TIME TO WASTE

The headline in the *Ithaca Daily News*, March 4, 1903. Soper's middle initial was actually "A."

As his train made its way to Ithaca, George Soper peered out at the rolling hills, picturesque farms, and the occasional small towns of upstate New York. To some,

DR. GEORGE H. SOPER HERE TO INVESTIGATE EPIDEMIC

it might have seemed an unlikely area in which to find an epidemic. But Soper knew that just one condition was needed for typhoid to spread: a single person excreting the bacteria.

When he stepped off the train at the Ithaca station that evening, he learned that the total number of sick had risen to 600. Six new cases had been reported that day, and four more were suspected. Nineteen Cornell students were dead and at least that many Ithacans. To Soper, it seemed like a "city . . . in a condition bordering on panic."

Ithacans enthusiastically welcomed him because they'd heard about his reputation. The former president of the New York City Board of Health had called him "a competent, experienced, energetic man." Leaders from the medical community had lauded his abilities as a sanitation engineer in the *New York Times* and the *Journal of the American Medical Association*.

Upon hearing that Soper was in charge of the Ithaca cleanup, a respected bacteriologist wrote: "It is certainly one of the hopeful signs of the times that a man of practical experience and energy, combined with scientific knowledge, should be placed in a position of authority."

With thousands of lives at stake, Soper promptly went to work. The night he arrived, he met with Ithaca's health officer to ask questions about the outbreak. The next day, he requested a tour of the city so that he could check out its sanitary conditions.

In a meeting on Wednesday evening, Soper warned Ithaca's board of health, the city council, and representatives from Cornell that "the city stood in great peril and that drastic measures must be instituted to save it." If they didn't act now, he told them, the epidemic might continue for months or even years.

Typhoid patients would pass the bacteria on to people who hadn't been made ill by the initial water contamination. Ithaca had to be sanitized as soon as possible and, Soper emphasized, definitely before spring. Warm weather would bring flies that could spread bacteria from the feces of infected patients.

The city council immediately voted to spend as much money as necessary to stop the typhoid outbreak.

Tall and handsome with dark hair and a mustache, George Soper impressed Ithaca's residents when he spoke. After he made an appearance before the general public at the Music Hall, a local newspaper reported: "Dr. Soper is an earnest, learned and convincing speaker, and was most attentively listened to by the hundreds of persons present."

Ithacans finally felt relief. This expert would help their city be healthy again.

KEEP BOILING

Soper set out to investigate the likely source of the epidemic—Ithaca's water supply. Walking along the two creeks that provided water to the city and the one used by the university, he looked for places where human waste might have seeped into the streams. He saw plenty.

Scores of outhouses sat on the creek banks. Their contents oozed into the running water and turned the streams into sewers. On farms along the creeks, Soper discovered that men sometimes defecated in manure piles instead of in a privy. Rain and melting snow washed their waste into the nearby stream.

In the months before the outbreak, at least six people living along the creeks had been diagnosed with typhoid fever. Any of them might have been the original source of the epidemic. In one home, the excrement of a typhoid

Opposite top: In a photograph from Soper's report on the Ithaca epidemic, houses, barns, and outhouses line the banks of Six Mile Creek, polluting the city's water supply.

Opposite bottom: An undated cartoon shows flies carrying human and animal waste to the table from an outhouse, manure pile, and barn. Soper warned that flies could spread typhoid germs.

TRANSMISSION *of* INTESTINAL DISEASES *by* FLIES

TO SWAT

Time Flies

victim had been dumped in the snow on the creek's bank. As the snow melted, the waste drained into the water headed to Ithaca.

Soper talked to Ithaca's health department and learned that Six Mile Creek was considered the source of the outbreak. Many Ithacans blamed a team of sixty Italian immigrants who had worked along it. During the weeks before the epidemic began, the men had been building a dam for the water company. Sanitation at their camp had been poor, and some of them had defecated on the creek banks.

Soper found no medical reports of any workers having typhoid fever. Because they had since left town, he couldn't verify that the Italian workers had been the source of the typhoid bacteria.

After examining the water supply, Soper concluded: "Among such a large number of sources of pollution as were obvious, it was difficult to discriminate. Any one of over a dozen might have been the cause."

Although the original contamination by typhoid bacteria was probably over, testing showed that city water remained polluted. Soper warned Ithacans to keep boiling it.

As a permanent solution, he endorsed the city's plan to install a filtration system. Soper had seen typhoid rates plummet in cities after they started to filter their drinking water. By percolating water through large beds of sand, these systems removed bacteria that caused waterborne diseases such as typhoid fever, dysentery, and diarrhea. Work on Ithaca's new filtration system began at the end of March.

DESTROYING THE INVISIBLE

Meanwhile, the sick continued to lose their battle with the typhoid bacteria. On March 13, Cornell junior Schuyler

Moore died at his widowed mother's house a few miles up Cayuga Lake from Ithaca. "His death is deeply deplored," a local newspaper said, "for it was believed that he had an excellent career before him." Another life had been cut short on the verge of adulthood.

Even though the number of new cases had tapered off, Soper worried that the epidemic might still spread from the existing patients. He told the city council: "We are dealing with an enemy that moves in the dark. We cannot see the bacteria, and can only destroy them by cleaning and disinfecting the places where we believe them to exist."

He recommended careful disinfection of every patient's body waste and bedclothes as well as the outhouse or toilet where excrement was dumped. At his suggestion, the city hired twenty men who used four horse-drawn wagons to deliver the disinfecting chemicals—lime chloride and mercury chloride—to homes of typhoid patients. Soper made sure that residents also received printed instructions for using the disinfectants.

Caregivers were advised to wash their hands frequently so that they didn't ingest bacteria or pass them on to others. When Dr. Alice Potter caught typhoid from one of her patients, Ithacans saw how contagious the lethal disease was. Three weeks later, the popular thirty-three-year-old physician died.

CLEAN THE CITY

Soper next turned his attention to the unsanitary conditions he had seen during his first tour of the city. Although Ithaca had a sewage system, many homeowners instead used their own outhouses or cesspools. Soper discovered that these were overflowing with "millions of typhoid germs."

A team of fifteen men was hired to clean out and disinfect the 1,200 outhouses and 300 cesspools in the city. Horse-drawn wagons hauled 418,000 gallons of human waste to a field outside of town. It was plowed into twelve acres of ground to decompose.

Many Ithacans drew their drinking water from the 1,300 private wells in the city. Soper ordered testing to be sure they didn't harbor bacteria. Nearly a third of these wells turned out to be so contaminated that he condemned them.

In one case, dirty water sickened 50 people and killed 5. They had all been drinking from a neighbor's well in order to avoid the typhoid-carrying city water. Soper discovered that a leaky drainpipe from the house's toilet ran close to the well and carried waste into the drinking water.

The well's owner had been ill with what her doctor called grippe. A blood test later showed that she had typhoid fever. The woman, who generously shared her well water, unknowingly spread the disease to her neighbors with deadly results.

George Soper found out that most of the infected college students lived and ate their meals in boardinghouses. Male students stayed off campus because Cornell provided dormitory rooms only for women. He had each of the dozens of boardinghouses inspected, with a focus on the plumbing, inside bathrooms, and water supply. Owners were told how to fix sanitation problems. The boardinghouses that passed reinspection received a permit to operate.

Ithacans respected Soper's advice. One student, reluctant to return to Cornell until the risk of disease was gone, wrote President Schurman: "Do you think that . . . there is any great danger of secondary infection? Could you inform me what Dr. Soper's opinion is on this question?"

THE EPIDEMIC ENDS

At seven in the morning of May 6, the twenty-ninth Cornell student died. Leslie Atwater had grown up in Ithaca and was well liked for his "pleasing, generous disposition." His many friends were devastated by his death. A "bright light goes out," lamented the *Ithaca Daily News*. Leslie was officially the last Cornell student to die in the epidemic. He was less than two months from graduating.

The frightening, sorrowful months of disease and death pushed the university and city to make changes. Cornell decided to build dormitories for male students so that they would not be forced to live in the city's boardinghouses. The university built its own filtration plant to clean the water it pumped from one of the three local creeks.

Ithacans voted to take public control of the city's water system away from the private company whose bad management many blamed for the outbreak. New regulations banned sewage from being dumped into local streams. The city set standards for building and maintaining outhouses.

At the end of August 1903, more than seven months after the epidemic started, Ithaca's new filtration plant was in place. George Soper assured residents that the new system would "eliminate 97 or 98 per cent of bacteria" and "the water will be acceptably pure." Homeowners noticed the difference. "When I took my bath this morning," said one, "the water was as clear as a whistle."

By September 1, Soper's work was finished. The bill for six months of his services was about $2,300. This was a substantial fee when the average annual household income in New York State was $675. Commissioner of Health

A photograph of Cornell senior Leslie Atwater appeared in the Class Book of 1903, but he died before he could graduate.

Lewis pointed out to Ithaca's leaders that "all sanitarians who are familiar with Dr. Soper's qualifications . . . regard his services as cheap at any price."

The cost of cleaning up the city, including the filtration system, totaled more than $100,000.

A PRICE TOO HIGH

The victims of the epidemic owed enormous bills for doctors, nursing care, and medicine. The cost of three months of care for one patient could be $450 or more, an amount difficult for most families to pay.

City residents had to deal with these expenses themselves. Fortunately for the hundreds of Cornell

Steel industrialist Andrew Carnegie (1835–1919) and his wife, Louise, around 1908. Both had survived typhoid fever.

students who suffered, a wealthy member of the university's board of trustees, industrialist Andrew Carnegie, paid their bills.

Carnegie understood typhoid's toll because it had almost killed him earlier in his life. Several years later, the disease left his wife so weak that she couldn't walk for three months. Carnegie donated tens of thousands of dollars to pay for student medical bills and for the university's new filtration system.

The cost in lost and damaged lives was incalculable. About 1 in 10 Ithacans—1,350 victims—developed typhoid fever and spent long months recovering. Of those, 82 died, including 29 Cornell students.

George Soper believed that the actual total would never be confirmed.

Recordkeeping had been incomplete, and an unknown number of people connected to the outbreak had died elsewhere. Some students infected in Ithaca went home and spread the disease to family members, who became ill and died.

The typhoid epidemic left countless broken hearts. A widow visited Cornell's president after her son died. She told Jacob Schurman that the young student had been "the sole stay of her declining years." Now she was alone.

Theodore Zinck, a German immigrant who owned a downtown bar popular with Cornell students, became a victim even though he was never sick. His only child, twenty-four-year-old Louise, was struck down during the first weeks of the outbreak. She seemed to be improving, but she took a turn for the worse and died on February 24. That summer, after enduring four months of unbearable grief, Theodore rowed a boat into the middle of Cayuga Lake and drowned himself.

In Soper's view, the tragic epidemic should have been prevented before a single Ithacan fell ill. He later said, "Seldom has so terrible a lesson of the consequences of sanitary neglect been given."

He was determined to stop this from happening again in a different town to other innocent victims.

MYSTERIOUS OUTBREAK

"All the skill of an expert detective is often required . . . to discover the exact manner and the exact route by which typhoid fever was actually conveyed from one person to another."
—William Sedgwick

I n the summer of 1906, New York banker Charles Henry Warren rented a spacious country house in Oyster Bay, a village on Long Island. Located in a neighborhood of beautiful homes, the house was surrounded by gardens, lawns, and porches. It was the perfect place for the Warren family to enjoy a relaxing summer away from the city's stifling heat, humidity, and foul odors.

The rich and powerful were drawn to Oyster Bay, particularly after Theodore Roosevelt became president in 1901. Roosevelt had vacationed in the town when he was a teen in the 1870s. As an adult, he built a house there, which he called Sagamore Hill. The Roosevelt family had made it their home since the mid-1880s, and now it was the summer White House.

But the Warren family's idyllic summer in famous Oyster Bay took an unexpected and alarming turn. On August 27, a rainy Monday near the end of their stay, the

Top: The Warren family of New York City rented this Oyster Bay house during the summer of 1906.

Bottom: In 1905, President Theodore Roosevelt (1858–1919) plays with his dogs at Sagamore Hill, his house in Oyster Bay. Roosevelt was president from 1901 to 1909.

Warrens' daughter became feverish and weak. A doctor was called immediately, and he broke the bad news: she had typhoid fever. The family was shocked and dismayed, yet more was to come.

Within a week, Mrs. Warren, a second daughter, two maids, and a gardener fell ill. Out of 11 family members and servants staying in the house, 6 developed the awful typhoid symptoms. Two were so sick that they had to be taken to the hospital, though none of the victims died.

Such an outbreak was rare in Oyster Bay. No other cases occurred during the months before and after the Warren household became ill. Typhoid fever seemed to be centered on that single house.

In September, the owners of the house, Mr. and Mrs. George Thompson of New York City, hired inspectors to examine the property and its water supply. The results revealed no definite explanation for the outbreak.

This wasn't good enough for the Thompsons. Their house was an investment, and they planned to rent it again. With the cloud of typhoid fever hanging over it, the house might as well have a quarantine sign on the front door.

The Thompsons wanted to find out the cause of the outbreak and fix it. That required hiring a first-rate expert, someone with the reputation to assure potential renters that the house posed no danger.

They contacted George Soper.

THE SEARCH FOR ANSWERS

After completing his work in Ithaca in 1903, Soper had continued to build his reputation as "an epidemic fighter." He investigated typhoid outbreaks throughout the Northeast and advised stricken communities on ways to end their epidemics and prevent new ones. Desperate to solve the mystery of their Oyster Bay house, the Thompsons gladly paid his fee.

Soper's first step in solving the Thompsons' problem was to gather as much information as possible. Several weeks had passed since the outbreak, but he was able to review the earlier inspection results. Next, he took the train from Manhattan to Oyster Bay to examine the scene for himself.

When he arrived, he checked the usual causes of typhoid outbreaks, as he had in Ithaca. "The most important question," Soper later wrote, "was how the first case occurred."

The Warrens reported that nobody who became ill had been away from the village all summer. Soper interviewed the three doctors who practiced in Oyster Bay. They confirmed that the only cases they had seen were in the Warren household.

Focusing on the house, Soper studied the most common source of typhoid bacteria, the water supply. The drinking water came from a deep well on the property. It was a safe distance from the servants' outhouse and from two cesspools that collected waste from the family's indoor toilet. All had been cleaned out in the spring, just a few months before the outbreak. Soper read the water purity reports made by two separate laboratories shortly after the outbreak. The results came back clean with no bacteria.

If the water supply wasn't the source, maybe typhoid bacteria had been in the household's food. Soper asked the Warrens about their diet that summer. The family's milk came from the same dairy used by other residents of Oyster Bay. That eliminated typhoid-contaminated milk, which often caused outbreaks.

Another possibility was that raw foods, such as fruits

and vegetables, carried the bacteria. But everyone in the household—those who became sick and those who didn't—apparently ate the same food. Still, as Soper had seen in other outbreaks, people who were exposed didn't always develop typhoid. Perhaps they hadn't ingested enough of the germs, or they had immunity due to a previous attack.

One of the Warrens mentioned how much they all loved clams. At last, Soper thought he might have found the culprit. Shellfish from polluted waters sometimes contained typhoid bacteria.

When he asked more questions, he discovered that no one had eaten clams or other shellfish for six weeks before the disease struck. That was too long to have caused the typhoid fever cases. Soper had to throw out this hypothesis.

A CLUE SURFACES

So far, he couldn't lay the blame on any of the typical sources of typhoid bacteria. But Soper wasn't someone who gave up easily.

Keeping in mind typhoid fever's incubation period, he asked the Warrens: Did anything unusual happen one to three weeks before their daughter—the first victim—became sick? Did anyone in the household have typhoid symptoms earlier in the summer?

No, they answered to both questions.

The Warrens recalled one thing, however. They had changed cooks during the first week of August.

Interesting, thought Soper. He realized that the timing was significant—three weeks before the first person showed symptoms. He asked what they knew about the cook.

Her name was Mary Mallon, the Warrens told him. She was Irish, about forty years old, and an intelligent woman.

They had hired her through an employment agency, and she came with fine recommendations. Pleased with the food she prepared, they paid her $45 a month, a good wage for a domestic servant. The family mentioned that Mary had prepared a delicious ice-cream dessert with fresh cut peaches.

She no longer worked for them, though. The cook had left the household a few weeks after their daughter fell ill.

Soper wondered if this woman had been the source of the bacteria. She handled the household's food every day. Most of it was heated, which killed the bacteria. But she likely touched uncooked foods, too, like fresh cut fruit. If she hadn't washed her hands after using the toilet, her fingers might have been covered with typhoid germs.

The Warrens said that Mary never became ill, so it didn't appear that she spread the disease while she was sick. At the very least, thought Soper, the cook might be able to help him figure out the cause of the outbreak.

TRACKING MARY

The Warrens had no idea where Mary Mallon had gone after leaving Oyster Bay. Several weeks had passed. She could be anywhere, even out of the area. Soper had only one lead to go on: the employment agency that had sent her to the Warrens.

When he spoke to the agency's owner, the man couldn't guess where Mary Mallon was working now. But he was willing to give Soper a list of her references stretching back several years.

Soper started to work his way down the list of names. At each household, he asked for information about Mallon, including whether anyone had typhoid while she was cooking there.

A chef works in the kitchen of a wealthy New York City family in 1899. During this period, Mary Mallon was cooking in similar kitchens for well-to-do New Yorkers.

Mallon's employers told him that they had been satisfied with her and considered her a competent cook. She seemed to have no problem finding jobs with well-to-do families.

Soper also interviewed housekeepers and other servants. Did they know where he could find her? Few remembered much about Mallon, or they didn't want to tell him. He suspected they were protecting her. "Servants who had been associated with her never gave any help," Soper later recalled.

Eventually, he traced her employment history back ten years. In 1897, he learned, a New York City family hired Mallon as their cook. During the summer of 1900, she accompanied them to their vacation home in Mamaroneck, about thirty miles north of Manhattan.

When Soper asked about typhoid fever, the family recalled that a visitor had come to stay at the end of August. Within ten days, the young man developed typhoid. A few days later, Mary Mallon left her job.

Soper picked up her trail again in 1901–02 when, for eleven months, she worked for another family in New York City. A month after Mallon began cooking there, a laundress in the household became so ill with typhoid fever that she had to be hospitalized.

By the summer of 1902, Mallon had moved on again. A lawyer from New York City, J. Coleman Drayton, hired her to travel with his family to their Maine vacation home as the summer cook. The household included 4 family members, 4 servants, and Mallon.

In mid-June, a servant came down with typhoid fever. Before long, 7 of the 9 in the house became sick, as well as a local nurse and servant who came in each day to help.

Mr. Drayton was spared, perhaps because he had immunity after a previous typhoid attack. Mary Mallon didn't become ill either. She volunteered to help Drayton care for the sick, and he paid her a $50 bonus for her trouble. No other typhoid cases occurred in the Maine community that summer. Tests of the house's water supply found it safe.

THE TRAIL GETS WARMER

Soper couldn't pinpoint where Mallon had worked in the months after leaving the Drayton family in 1902. But his search led to another New York City family, the Gilseys, who employed Mallon in 1904.

After she had cooked for the Gilseys for nine months, she went with them to their Sands Point, Long Island, summer home. Within three weeks, 4 people living in the separate servants' cottage were struck with typhoid fever. One, a laundress, became severely ill, but she survived. None of the victims had worked with Mary Mallon before. An investigation at the time of the outbreak found no contaminated drinking water.

Soper lost the cook's trail for nearly two years until 1906, when she ended up in Oyster Bay with the Warrens.

After Mallon left there in September 1906, she took a job with the Kesslers in Tuxedo Park, New York, about forty miles north of New York City. Two weeks later, the family's laundress was taken to the hospital with typhoid. Local health officials reported that there had been no typhoid fever in the town for several years.

Soper was too late to find Mallon with the Kesslers. She had left the job in October, two weeks after the laundress became sick.

After four months, George Soper had uncovered several outbreaks of typhoid fever connected to Mary Mallon. Only a few had been studied at the time they occurred. In most of those, the blame for the outbreak was put on the first victim, who investigators believed caught the disease outside the household. They never figured out where any of these people originally picked up the typhoid bacteria.

Soper wasn't convinced by this explanation. He had a hunch that Mallon was the key to all these outbreaks.

In early February 1907, he got a tip. After Mallon left Tuxedo Park the previous fall, she had taken a job in New York City. Walter Bowne and his family lived in a brownstone house at 688 Park Avenue in a wealthy neighborhood. Mary Mallon was their new cook.

Soper had finally tracked her down.

A THREAT TO THE CITY

"We have here, in my judgment, a case of a chronic typhoid germ distributor." —George Soper

The satisfaction George Soper felt in finding Mary Mallon soon disappeared. Two members of the Bowne household had recently become victims of typhoid fever. A female servant had been taken to the hospital. The second patient was one of the Bownes' two children, a twenty-five-year-old daughter named Effie, "a beautiful and talented girl."

Soper's investigation had revealed a disturbing pattern. He had traced eight of the households where Mallon worked in the previous ten years. In seven of them, someone developed typhoid fever while she was the cook—a total of 24 people. Yet even when other servants fell ill, she never did. The outbreaks had been the only typhoid cases at the time in those neighborhoods or communities.

The facts troubled Soper. Mary Mallon might be one

of the typhoid carriers that the German scientist Robert Koch had recently described. Despite being in good health, was she harboring typhoid bacteria in her body and spreading them to others?

From a scientific point of view, Soper realized this was an exciting discovery. Mallon was the first case of a healthy typhoid carrier ever found in the United States. But from a public health standpoint, it was chilling. "Under suitable conditions," he feared, "Mary might precipitate a great epidemic."

To confirm his suspicions, George Soper needed irrefutable proof that Mallon was the source of the outbreaks. It was possible that her connection to these cases had been an unfortunate coincidence. After all, typhoid fever was widespread in the New York area. In 1905, more than 4,300 cases and nearly 650 deaths had been confirmed in the city. Soper was sure there were many more that hadn't been correctly diagnosed or reported by doctors.

He saw just one way to prove that Mary Mallon was a carrier: test her body for typhoid bacteria.

Opposite: **A row of outhouses stands next to the water pump outside a New York City tenement house, around 1907. Typhoid bacteria spread easily under these conditions.**

TYPHOID FEVER.

This Notice is Posted in Compliance with Law

"Every person who shall wilfully tear down, remove or deface any notice posted in compliance with law, shall be fined not more than seven dollars."---GENERAL STATUTES OF CONNECTICUT, REVISION OF 1902, SECTION 1173.

Town Health Officer.

Fear of contagion led some communities to require a quarantine sign on a typhoid patient's house.

CONFRONTING THE COOK

Soper headed to the Bownes' Park Avenue home to talk to Mallon. He found her in the kitchen wearing a white apron. The stove warmed the room on the frosty February day.

A tall woman at five feet six inches, Mary Mallon had blue eyes and blond hair pulled back into a tight knot. She looked strong and healthy to Soper, perhaps even a bit overweight. She obviously was neither suffering with typhoid symptoms nor recovering from a recent bout.

He tried to be tactful when he explained the situation. He assumed she wondered why people kept getting typhoid fever wherever she worked. Hadn't it ever occurred to her that she might have something to do with the outbreaks?

This photograph, taken in 1900, shows the brownstone houses on the Park Avenue block where the Bowne family lived.

"I had to say I suspected her of making people sick," Soper recalled. It wasn't her fault, he assured her, but there was a good chance she was spreading typhoid through the food she prepared. He offered to show her how to stop infecting others by washing her hands and being careful with her excretions.

"I thought I could count upon her coöperation in clearing up some of the mystery which surrounded her past," he said later. He hoped Mallon would tell him about other places she'd worked.

"I wanted specimens of her urine, feces and blood," Soper remembered telling her. "If she would answer my questions and give me the specimens, I would see that she got good medical attention, in case that was called for, and without any cost to her."

George Soper was stunned by Mary Mallon's reaction to what he considered a reasonable request. With her eyes full of hostility, she chased the epidemic fighter out of her kitchen.

Seeing her fury, Soper took the hint and fled down the hallway and through the iron gate that led out to the sidewalk. "I felt rather lucky to escape," he later wrote, admitting that maybe he hadn't handled her very well.

THE SURPRISE VISIT

Frustrated, Soper decided to try a different approach to get Mallon's cooperation. He had to make her understand her role in the outbreaks. She didn't seem to appreciate how important it was to give him the information and specimens he needed.

By asking around, Soper discovered that Mallon had a boyfriend in Manhattan named A. Briehof. The man lived in a Third Avenue tenement room and spent his days in a bar on the nearby corner. Soper sought him out. He persuaded Briehof to alert him the next time Mallon was coming to visit. But Soper asked Briehof not to tell her about their conversation.

On the arranged evening, Soper went to the tenement. He took along his physician friend and former assistant from the Ithaca outbreak, Dr. Bert Raymond Hoobler. The plan was for Hoobler to help obtain the specimens.

The two climbed the staircase to Briehof's room on the top floor, where they waited. Soon they heard Mallon's footsteps on the stairs.

When she spotted George Soper at the top, she was first startled and then incensed.

Once again, Soper tried to explain that she might be spreading typhoid fever germs. He told her that he "meant her no harm." He just wanted a sample of her urine, feces, and blood for testing.

Soper's words only made Mary Mallon angrier. In her Irish brogue, she demanded to know how anyone could accuse her of such a thing. She was a clean person, couldn't they see? She worked for reputable employers who wouldn't hire someone who was dirty. She was healthy and always had been. She had nothing whatsoever to do with anyone catching typhoid. Why, in fact, five years ago she had put herself at risk to help *cure* the family at Mr. Drayton's Maine summer home.

George Soper saw that Mallon wasn't going to let him take the specimens. With her curses echoing in the stairwell, he and Hoobler retreated down the stairs and into the street, relieved to get away from the outraged woman.

DANGER TO THE COMMUNITY

On Saturday, February 23, after a two-week illness, Effie Bowne died. The funeral was held at the Bownes' home the following Tuesday morning. Soper later wrote that the family was "prostrated with grief" at the death of their only daughter.

Effie Bowne was the first fatality that Soper had connected to Mary Mallon, and it raised the stakes. In Ithaca and other cities, Soper had seen the misery brought on by typhoid. This cook could be a threat to every person with whom she had contact. He had tried to reason with her, but he'd failed. Someone with more authority would have to deal with her now.

Soper collected his evidence of Mallon's ten-year trail of typhoid fever. On Monday, March 11, 1907, he presented it all to Dr. Hermann Biggs, the general medical officer at the New York City Department of Health. Soper had worked as a sanitary engineer for the Department in 1902. He knew it had the legal power to examine the cook, even taking her into custody if she wouldn't voluntarily provide specimens for testing.

If Mary Mallon was a carrier, as Soper suspected, she was a "menace to the community." She had to be stopped.

Soper's list of twenty-four typhoid cases caused by Mallon. The list appeared in a document later submitted by the health department to a judge. The Bownes' name is misspelled.

places and dates of outbreaks of Typhoid Fever ascribed by Dr. Soper as being due to Typhoid bacilli carried by Mary Mallon.

Date	Place	Cases		Name of person asking for investigation.
Sept.4,1900	Marmaroneck, N.Y.	1	cures	
Dec. 9,1901	New York City,N.Y.	1	"	
June 17,1902	Dark Harbor, Me.	9	"	Coleman Drayton
" 1,1904	Sands Point, N. Y.	4	"	Henry Gilsey
Aug. 27,1906	Oyster Bay, N. Y.	6	"	George Thompson
Sept.21,1906	Tuxedo, N.Y.	1	"	George Kes
Jan. 23,1907	New York City, N.Y.	2	"	Bowen

The Healthy Carriers

By the end of the nineteenth century, scientists knew that typhoid fever was caused by bacteria spreading from human to human. But they wondered why typhoid suddenly appeared in areas where no one had been sick with it before. If there was no obvious source of the disease, such as contaminated water or food, how did the bacteria get there?

A clue came during the Spanish-American War of 1898. Typhoid fever broke out among almost every volunteer regiment in United States training camps, striking 1 in 5 soldiers. Yet not a single soldier with symptoms of the disease had been allowed into the camps.

After investigating, a team of U.S. Army doctors concluded that some soldiers who looked and felt healthy must have carried the typhoid bacteria. In their report, the doctors wrote that "the specific germ of this disease . . . when cast out in the stools [feces] may become a source of danger to others." Typhoid spread easily under the often unsanitary conditions in military camps.

Soon after, Robert Koch studied a typhoid outbreak in several German villages. He tested the excrement of residents, using new culturing methods that detected typhoid bacteria. He discovered the germs in people who were *not* sick.

In November 1902, Koch gave a speech to other scientists in Berlin during which he discussed healthy carriers of the typhoid bacteria. These people had recovered from typhoid fever or experienced such mild cases that they never knew they had it. In most patients, either the body's immune system destroys the bacteria or the patient dies. But in a carrier, the bacteria continue

German bacteriologist Robert Koch (1843–1910) was the first to isolate tuberculosis, anthrax, and cholera bacteria. He received the Nobel Prize in Physiology or Medicine in 1905.

Soldiers with typhoid fever lie in cots lined up at the American military hospital in Puerto Rico during the Spanish-American War of 1898.

to live and multiply and are periodically discharged in feces or urine.

By 1906, when George Soper began investigating the Oyster Bay outbreak, he had read Koch's speech. This led him to track down Mary Mallon, whom he suspected was a carrier.

Later studies showed that about half of typhoid patients give off the bacteria in their feces, and occasionally in their urine, for a month after recovering from symptoms. About 20 percent still shed the bacteria after two months, and 10 percent after three months.

Approximately 5 percent of recovered patients have *Salmonella* Typhi in their excrement more than a year after disease symptoms are gone. They are the chronic typhoid carriers. Three times as many women as men harbor the bacteria without becoming sick. Children rarely become carriers.

The bacteria usually settle in the gallbladder, where bile is stored. They may also be found in the bile ducts, liver, or kidneys. In some carriers, they remain there for decades, ready to infect others.

Typhoid carriers live, on average, as long as anyone else. But they are more likely to have gallstones and may be more susceptible to cancer of the gallbladder, bile duct, and pancreas. One carrier lived to be 101 years old, carrying the bacteria in her body for eighty years without becoming sick.

PURSUIT

"She came out fighting and swearing, both of which she could do with appalling efficiency and vigor."
—S. Josephine Baker

Hermann Biggs read the report on his desk with dismay. A typhoid carrier could threaten the city that he had worked so hard to protect.

Because the report came from George Soper, Biggs took it seriously. He knew all about Soper's work as an epidemiologist and sanitary engineer, including during the 1903 Ithaca outbreak.

Biggs had been born and raised near Ithaca, where he attended high school before entering Cornell University. His brother and uncle were Ithaca physicians who had seen the epidemic firsthand. This uncle had inspired Biggs to go to medical school in the early 1880s.

Hermann Biggs believed in a principle that drove him to devote his life to public health: "Disease is largely a removable evil." Now forty-seven, he had been the general medical officer for New York City's health department since 1902. Biggs had worked with each commissioner to build the best health department in the United States. It had to be.

Contagious diseases surged through the city's crowded tenements and shantytowns. The immigrant-filled neighborhoods were bulging with more than 200,000 people living in each square mile. That was the same number of residents in Minneapolis, Minnesota—a fifty-square-mile city.

Ten years before Biggs became the general medical officer, he established a bacteriology laboratory at the health department. Using the latest methods, the bacteriologists studied the microbes that caused lethal contagious diseases such as cholera, diphtheria, smallpox, and tuberculosis.

By identifying microorganisms found in the sick, the laboratory diagnosed diseases quickly. That helped the health department treat patients and control outbreaks.

This laboratory would test Mary Mallon for typhoid.

Hermann Biggs assigned the task of obtaining Mallon's body specimens to Dr. Walter Bensel, the man in charge of the health department's medical inspectors. Inspectors combed the city, on the watch for unhealthy people who should be treated or isolated before they infected anyone else.

Bensel decided that Mary Mallon might be more cooperative if a female inspector asked for her specimens. He had someone in mind, his assistant Dr. S. Josephine Baker.

Hermann Biggs (1859–1923) worked for the New York City health department for twenty-six years before becoming New York State's commissioner of health.

To combat the unsanitary conditions in New York's crowded neighborhoods, city workers clean up garbage piled in the street in the early 1900s.

JO

Sara Josephine Baker's life might have been different if Poughkeepsie, New York, had filtered its drinking water.

But instead of following the same path as her mother—attending Vassar College, marrying well, and having several children—Jo watched her life abruptly change direction when she was sixteen.

In spring 1890, Jo's prosperous lawyer father contracted typhoid fever and died. He wasn't the first, or the last, in the city to die that way. Typhoid outbreaks were common in Poughkeepsie, which was located on the Hudson River just below an insane asylum's sewer outlet.

Mr. Baker's death left Jo, her semi-invalid sister, and her mother with a house to live in but not enough savings to support them for long. Jo realized that it would be up to her to earn a living for her family when the cash ran out.

She decided that a professional career was the best way to bring in money. Attending Vassar College in Poughkeepsie was no longer an option. College would delay her professional training by several years.

She was never quite sure what led her to choose medicine. No one in the family had been a doctor, and "both sides of the family were aghast" at her plans. Few women went into medicine, and Jo knew "that the world did not wholly approve of them." She later said that when friends and family tried to talk her out of it, her stubbornness made her go ahead "at all costs and in spite of everyone."

Jo heard about a Manhattan school that accepted women—the Women's Medical College of the New York Infirmary. Most medical schools did not require a four-year college degree, and she was able to enroll with only her high-school education.

After paying her tuition with much of the money her father had left, Jo moved into a boardinghouse and prepared for classes to start. She worried that she'd made a mistake and wasted the family's savings. Yet once she began her medical studies, Jo knew that it was "the one thing of all others that I will and must do."

THE NEW DOCTOR

In the spring of 1898, twenty-four-year-old Dr. S. Josephine Baker graduated second in her class of eighteen. She headed to Boston for her internship.

While Baker was working at a clinic that served the Boston slums, she was called to deliver a baby. When she arrived at the tenement apartment, she found a woman in labor lying on a pile of straw. Four little children cowered nearby. The drunken husband was sprawled on the floor.

As Baker began attending to the mother, she noticed that the woman's back was badly burned. The woman told Baker "her husband had thrown a kettle of scalding water over her a few days before."

Shouting obscenities, the furious husband pushed himself up and staggered toward the young doctor. Baker had to do something about him, though he weighed twice as much as she did.

She ran toward the apartment door, and the man followed, yelling and cursing at her. When he came close enough, she punched him as hard as she could. Already nearly too drunk to stand, the man fell backward out of the apartment. Baker slammed the door behind him, blocked it with furniture, and delivered the baby.

Josephine Baker had come a long way from her quiet, privileged upbringing in Poughkeepsie.

When her Boston internship ended, Baker returned to New York City to start her own practice. Her former professors advised against it. They recommended moving to a smaller community, like her hometown of Poughkeepsie, where she'd find less competition for patients.

But Baker was determined. She had enjoyed living in

Manhattan while she was in school, and she wanted to stay. Disregarding the advice, she and a medical-school friend opened an office on New York's Upper West Side.

Being female physicians turned out to be an advantage. Many women preferred to be examined and treated by a woman doctor, and New York had few of them. Most of the families that came to the office, however, couldn't afford to pay much for their medical care. Baker struggled to make a living.

When Josephine Baker (1873–1945) began her medical practice, contagious diseases flourished among the millions of New Yorkers living in a small area. This Manhattan street scene was photographed in 1900.

Top: Students line up for lunch in a New York City school, around 1910. In her first job at the health department, Baker examined schoolchildren for contagious diseases.

Right: Baker took special interest in impoverished children, such as these four who lived in a Lower East Side tenement around 1910.

THE INSPECTOR

One day in 1901, she heard that New York City's health department was hiring medical inspectors. The salary was $30 a month, which sounded good to Baker after making half that rate in her medical practice. Since the position was only part-time, she would still be able to treat her own patients. Baker applied.

She was hired to inspect schoolchildren for head lice, eye infections, and contagious skin diseases such as ringworm and scabies. Before long, Baker became frustrated. She didn't have time to examine each child adequately, and she doubted that the infected children she sent home ever received the required follow-up visit by another inspector.

Baker discovered that the health department was full of political appointees who did little or no work. "It reeked of negligence and stale tobacco smoke and slacking," she observed with disgust. She vowed to quit and return to her medical practice full-time.

Then in November of 1901, a new mayor was elected. He appointed a different health commissioner and made Hermann Biggs the general medical officer. "The whole department shuddered at the shake-up and house-cleaning that occurred," Baker later wrote. She was pleased with the fresh dedication, efficiency, and honesty. When her new supervisor, Walter Bensel, offered to raise her salary to $100 a month, she decided to stay.

For the next few years, Baker was a roving medical inspector. She visited the tenements, where she often found a dozen people living in one room. "I climbed stair after stair, knocked on door after door, met drunk after drunk, filthy mother after filthy mother and dying baby after dying baby," she recalled. "There was no dodging

the hopelessness of it all."

She was shocked to learn that a third of slum children never lived to age five. Each week in the summer, 1,500 of the city's babies died, many from dysentery caused by drinking contaminated milk and water. Baker decided "that something could and must be done" about the "mass of misery." She didn't yet know how, but she would find a way to change these terrible conditions.

THE BROWNSTONE ON PARK AVENUE

On Monday, March 18, 1907—one week after George Soper alerted the health department—medical inspector Josephine Baker was on her way to visit the suspected typhoid carrier.

If the cook Mary Mallon was truly a carrier, Baker knew how crucial it was to test her. The health department had enough trouble controlling typhoid outbreaks caused by polluted water and food. The last thing the city needed was a silent human carrier added to its bubbling caldron of germs.

When Baker reached the Bowne home on Park Avenue, she asked to speak with the cook. She was shown to the kitchen where she found Mary Mallon hard at work. Baker's first impression was that Mary was "a clean, neat, obviously self-respecting Irishwoman."

Baker was used to discussing health matters with immigrants, many of whom distrusted government and hospitals. She was careful in her choice of words so that she didn't sound accusing or threatening. But there was no way around bluntly asking for a sample of the cook's blood and urine.

Mary Mallon's response was clear and definite: "No."

Her glowering eyes and firm voice told Baker that no amount of coaxing or reasoning would change Mallon's

Sara Josephine Baker around the time she went to see Mary Mallon. Baker was called Josephine, and she usually used her first initial as part of her professional name. As a medical inspector, Baker visited neighborhoods where people lived under unsanitary conditions.

Opposite top: Garbage clutters the street in front of run-down apartments. *Opposite bottom:* Children play in a filthy tenement backyard next to outhouses. Both photographs were taken in 1912.

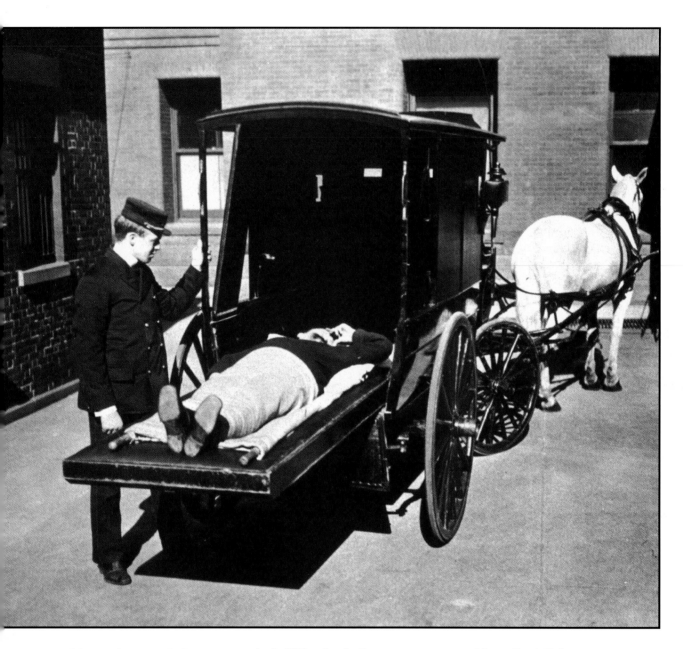

A horse-drawn ambulance used in New York City during the early 1900s

mind. Why hadn't anyone warned her that this woman might resist the testing request?

Empty-handed, Baker returned to the New York City Department of Health on Sixth Avenue. Walter Bensel repeated his instructions: Mary Mallon absolutely *must* provide specimens of her blood and urine for typhoid testing. He told Baker to go back to the brownstone the next day. Bensel arranged for an ambulance and some policemen to go with her this time. He said that "if Mary resisted, [they] were to take her to the Willard Parker Hospital, by force if necessary."

THE CHASE

The next morning dawned with snow and dampness in the air, the most miserable kind of weather that March could offer. Baker pulled on a warm coat and headed back to Park Avenue.

By 7:30 a.m., she had arrived at a corner near the Bowne house where the horse-drawn ambulance was already waiting. She hoped that Mallon would cooperate when she saw the policemen.

In case she didn't, Baker thought it wise to cut off possible escape routes. She sent one of the three officers to the front of the house and another to the closest side street. Then she and the third policeman approached the servants' entrance and knocked.

When the cook opened the door, she held a long, sharp kitchen fork. For a moment, Baker wondered whether Mary Mallon had been waiting for them.

Suddenly, Mallon thrust the fork toward her. Startled, Baker fell back against the policeman to avoid being stabbed. She realized that "this seemingly simple task" of obtaining specimens was going to be anything but easy.

By the time Baker and the policeman had pushed inside, Mallon was out of sight. The two gave chase. Backed by the legal authority of the health and police departments, they went room to room, looking behind furniture and in closets.

They couldn't find her, and no one in the household had seen her. Somehow, Mary Mallon had slipped out of the Bowne house.

While checking the backyard, Baker spotted their first clue: footprints in the snow. The prints led to a fence against which a chair had been propped. She noticed that the snow was brushed away on the top of the fence above the chair. Mallon must have climbed over into the neighboring yard.

Baker took the hunt to the brownstone next door. After explaining the situation to the neighbors, she and the officer searched that house, too, basement to attic. Baker asked the servants if the cook from next door had been there. Definitely not, they replied.

Mary Mallon had vanished. After nearly three hours of futile pursuit, Josephine Baker had failed in her assignment. She'd have to report to Dr. Bensel, and he wasn't going to like the news. Discouraged, Baker walked two blocks to Third Avenue, where she knew there was a telephone.

EVERY NOOK AND CRANNY

As she feared, her boss's response over the phone was short and to the point: "I expect you to get the specimens or to take Mary to the hospital."

Baker would have to try again. She figured that Mallon couldn't have gone far. The cook hadn't had time to grab a coat when she fled. And if she'd escaped to the street, the police officers would have seen her. For Baker to have any chance of finding Mallon, she needed more help.

On the way back to the Bownes' brownstone, Baker saw two other policemen on the street, and she took them with her. With these extra men joining in, Baker and the officers searched inside both houses again. "For another two hours we went through every closet and nook and cranny," Baker later recalled. "It was utter defeat."

As they were leaving through the basement door of the

second house, one of the officers nudged Baker. He pointed to a small outside closet under the front stairway. A piece of blue cotton fabric was stuck in the door. They hadn't noticed the colorful fragment before because it was partly hidden behind several ash cans piled in front of the closet.

The policeman moved the cans away and yanked open the door. A blond woman wearing a blue dress and white apron was crouched in the closet. Mary Mallon.

"She came out fighting and swearing, both of which she could do with appalling efficiency and vigor," Baker wrote later.

She ignored the cook's rage. She had a job to do. The health department needed to test Mallon for typhoid fever. Baker told the woman it was very important for her to provide urine and blood samples.

Mallon loudly and adamantly refused. Why were they persecuting her? She didn't have typhoid and never had. Why didn't they believe her?

With the woman in this agitated state, Baker knew she couldn't get the samples. They would have to take Mallon to Willard Parker, the contagious-disease hospital near the East River.

Mallon yelled and kicked as the policemen carried her to the ambulance and forced her inside. Even after the doors closed, she kept fighting.

With Mallon thrashing and screaming, Baker sat on top of the woman's body to keep her from breaking away. The bumpy three-mile ride downtown to the hospital felt to Josephine Baker "like being in a cage with an angry lion."

She didn't mind. The chase was over, and they had caught Mary Mallon.

A bacteriologist works in a laboratory around 1910.

People with scarlet fever, measles, and diphtheria were brought to Willard Parker. There they were isolated from the public so that they didn't set off an epidemic. The brick hospital had about two hundred beds, but it sometimes had three times as many patients.

Now that they finally had Mary Mallon, the health department officials wasted no time checking her for typhoid. The tests would be carried out by the Bureau of Laboratories, headed by Dr. William Park.

Park's interest in typhoid fever and the bacteria that caused it was both professional and personal. During the summer of 1896, he had been sick for several weeks with typhoid. Park blamed himself for being careless. While on a long bike ride about fifty miles northwest of the city, he became extremely thirsty and drank from a lake. The water turned out to be contaminated.

Under Park's direction, bacteriologists in the laboratory tested Mallon's urine and blood for typhoid. They also took samples of her feces, put them in an incubator, and examined the bacteria that grew.

The test results surprised Park and others in the health department. Her urine contained no typhoid bacteria. Many physicians believed urine was a major way that the bacteria spread.

The Widal blood test revealed a different story. It showed that Mallon's body contained antibodies against typhoid bacteria.

When Park saw the test results on her feces, he was astounded. The samples were teeming with typhoid bacteria. Mary Mallon, he said, was "a human 'culture tube.'"

George Soper's suspicions had been correct.

Doctors at the hospital gave Mallon a physical exam, looking for symptoms of typhoid fever. Just as Soper and Baker concluded when they first saw her, Mallon was healthy and "rosy-cheeked," looking nothing like a sick or recovering typhoid patient.

Even though Mallon didn't appear to have typhoid fever, the lab tests showed that the bacteria had definitely entered her body earlier in her life. She either didn't remember having symptoms or had suffered a mild case. It was also possible that she was lying when she said she had never had typhoid.

What mattered to the health department was that those dangerous bacteria were still inside her, reproducing and being shed in her feces. Baker's boss, Walter Bensel, called Mallon a "living fever factory."

During the early 1900s, surgery was less hygienic than it is today. In this operating room in 1900, no one wears a mask.

NOW WHAT?

The New York City Department of Health was holding the nation's first healthy typhoid carrier. But as Walter Bensel commented, "The Lord only knows what we can do with the woman."

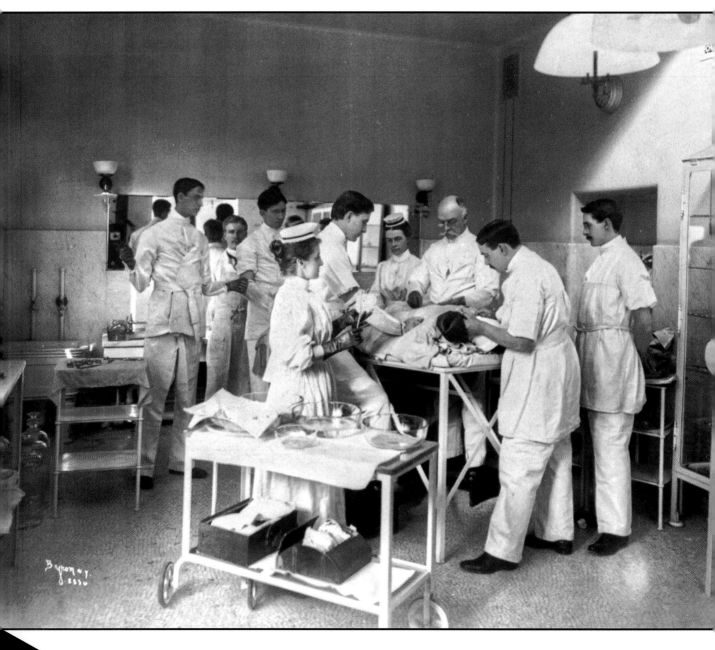

How could they prevent Mallon from infecting anyone else? No one had yet discovered a treatment guaranteed to destroy the typhoid bacteria inside a carrier's body.

European researchers had found typhoid bacteria in the gallbladder during operations to remove gallstones and during autopsies of carriers. Based on that discovery, some physicians claimed that they could cure a carrier by taking out his gallbladder.

But the surgery was controversial. Cautious doctors warned that it might not work. Typhoid bacteria likely hid in other parts of the body, too. And any surgery was risky and could lead to infection, bleeding, or other side effects that might kill the patient.

The doctors at Willard Parker thought it was worth a try, anyway. They asked Mallon if they could perform the surgery.

She refused. These people were not going to cut her open and take out her insides.

PEEP SHOW

The laboratory's results turned Mary Mallon's life into a nightmare. She knew they were wrong. She felt perfectly healthy. How could she be full of millions of germs?

Yet the doctors acted as if she had some strange, new disease. They asked her the same questions over and over again. Had she ever had typhoid fever? No! Had she been aware that she was making people sick? No!

The hospital moved her from the wards to a private room, where even more doctors crowded around her bed, discussing her case. Mallon was outraged. "I have been in fact a peep show for Evrey [sic] body," she complained.

Her room was drab and sterile, and she hated staying there. Hospital attendants guarded the door to stop her from escaping. The walls were white, the floors were white, the ceiling was white. It was a white prison.

About two weeks after Mallon had been dragged to Willard Parker Hospital, a couple of New York newspapers picked up her story. According to them, an Irish cook was being held by the health department. Her name was Mary Ilverson, and she was "a human vehicle for typhoid germs."

When reporters interviewed Walter Bensel, he explained why she'd been detained: "This woman is a great menace to health, a danger to the community, and she has been made a prisoner on that account."

The health department hid Mallon's real identity and the names of the "prominent families" to whom she passed the typhoid germs. One of the newspapers incorrectly said that the cook was being held prisoner at Roosevelt Hospital. The other stated she was in Bellevue Hospital.

But on one point, the articles about Mary were accurate. "Her language is far from cordial or gentle," wrote the reporter, "when the doctors visit her and talk of her internal storehouse of germs."

AN OFFER OF HELP

One day, Mary Mallon had an uninvited visitor to her white prison. She wasn't happy to see him. What did Dr. George Soper want with her now? Because of him, the health department had grabbed her and locked her up in this hospital.

Soper immediately started talking. He'd been right, he told her. The lab results proved that she had once had typhoid. She should stop denying the truth and being so stubborn. That's what had gotten her arrested in the first place.

Mallon stared at him, her anger growing. Soper seemed to be gloating.

"Many people have been made sick and have suffered

a great deal; some have died," he continued. He told her that none of it would have happened if she had washed her hands after using the toilet. "You don't keep your hands clean enough," he scolded.

Glaring, Mallon said nothing.

Soper went on with his speech, claiming that he could get her out of the hospital. He urged her to start cooperating and let the doctors take out her gallbladder. It was the best way to get rid of the germs. "You don't need a gallbladder any more than you need an appendix," he said.

Soper leaned against the door as he explained what he could do to help her. He intended to write a book about her case so that others would learn about typhoid carriers. Would Mary tell him when she'd had typhoid, where she'd worked, and who else might have gotten the fever from her? He promised not to use her real name, and he'd give her the profits from book sales.

Mallon had heard enough. Seething, she wrapped her white robe around her body, crossed the floor to the bathroom, and slammed the door shut.

QUARANTINE ISLAND

Several times a week, the laboratory tested Mallon's feces. The typhoid bacteria were still there. With her body shedding deadly germs, the doctors believed she remained a threat to the city. The health department had held Mallon in isolation against her will for about a month. Nothing could stop it from keeping her longer.

Since 1866, the New York City Board of Health had had broad powers. Out of concern about a cholera epidemic, the New York State Legislature had given the Board the authority to do whatever was necessary to protect the city's health. That included using the police to enforce quarantines and isolation of infected people. Health officials didn't need court permission to act.

Josephine Baker later observed: "There is very little that a Board of Health cannot do in the way of interfering with personal and property rights for the protection of the public health."

Officials decided to use that power to keep Mary Mallon in custody. But they'd have to find somewhere else to put her. Willard Parker Hospital needed Mallon's room for other patients.

The health department operated a quarantine hospital on North Brother Island in the middle of the East River. Riverside Hospital, built in the 1880s, had once been used to isolate people with highly contagious diseases such as typhus and smallpox.

In 1903, due to the efforts of Hermann Biggs, Riverside instead became a sanatorium for tuberculosis victims. The hospital treated patients who were expected to recover. It also held some people under "forcible detention" because they couldn't be trusted to stop spreading their tuberculosis germs.

Mary Mallon was to be the Island's first typhoid case under forcible detention. The only way on and off was by boat. They weren't going to keep her behind bars, but as far as Mary was concerned, North Brother Island was a jail.

Opposite: In an illustration from *Harper's Weekly*, September 1885, an angel holds a "cleanliness" shield against deadly diseases entering the Port of New York. Health officials quarantined incoming immigrants to control the spread of many diseases.

"THE MOST DANGEROUS WOMAN IN AMERICA"

"No knife will be put on me." —Mary Mallon

The ferry ride across the polluted East River to North Brother Island covered a quarter of a mile. Mallon felt as if she were being taken thousands of miles away from her world.

She'd heard of North Brother Island from the headlines. Three years before, in June 1904, the steamship the *General Slocum* burned and sank nearby. About 1,400 German Americans had been onboard, most of them women and children heading to a church picnic. More than a thousand of them died, and their bodies washed up on the Island's shore.

People had been dying there for years. North Brother Island was a place where you were sent to die, away from your family and friends. Being on the Island made Mallon feel "nervous & almost prostrated with greif [*sic*] & trouble." She didn't belong. She wasn't sick, and she wasn't dying.

The kidney-shaped island covered about twenty acres, less than the area of four blocks in Manhattan. It contained

a few trees, a church, a red-and-white lighthouse, some concrete buildings and wooden cottages, and the brick hospital full of tuberculosis patients. Mallon was glad they didn't make her stay in there.

Instead, they put her in a cottage at the southern end of the island that had once been the head nurse's home. The building wasn't large, but its many windows made it bright—definitely an improvement over the cramped room they'd locked her in at Willard Parker Hospital. She had a living area with a bed, table, small kitchen, and a bathroom with modern plumbing.

The cottage sat near the riverbank next to the church. From the porch, Mallon could see the buildings of Manhattan, where she'd once lived and worked . . . and now was forbidden to go.

BACTERIA FIGHTING

The health department doctors continued to monitor the typhoid bacteria in Mallon's body. At first, they asked her to provide samples of her feces three times a week for testing in the department's laboratory. She was relieved when, in November 1907, they cut back to once a week. But that didn't make her any less indignant about the way she was being treated.

They told her that they were trying to cure her. If they succeeded, they'd be able to release her, knowing that she couldn't infect others.

Off and on, the doctors gave her urotropin, a drug used

Left: Wrapped in blankets, survivors of the *General Slocum* disaster stand in front of Riverside Hospital on North Brother Island. Doctors, nurses, and other employees saved many from drowning.

Right: Bodies are lined up on the Island's shore.

to cure urinary-tract infections. The idea was that the drug would kill the bacteria in Mallon's bladder before the urine left her body.

When the urotropin didn't seem to reduce the amount of bacteria that Mallon shed, the doctors stopped giving it to her. Good thing, too, because the side effects made her miserable. "If I should have continued," she complained later, "it would certainly have killed me for it was very severe."

Next, the doctors tried several drugs that destroyed other types of microbes. They fed her brewer's yeast because it seemed to cure various ills. They changed her diet and gave her laxatives, hoping that would help. Nothing worked. At times, her feces were free of typhoid bacteria for as long as three or four weeks. But the microbes always reappeared.

Mallon couldn't trust the doctors. They didn't seem to know what they were doing or care about her. Their sole concern was the germs they claimed she carried. When her left eyelid became paralyzed, she asked them for help. No one did anything. After six months, the eyelid got better. In Mallon's opinion, it was "thanks to the Almighty God," not the doctors.

WHAT ABOUT THE OTHERS?

Mary Mallon's capture and imprisonment raised new questions for the health department. Investigators had been lucky to find her, but surely she wasn't the only healthy typhoid carrier walking around the city.

The Europeans thought that 5 percent of typhoid patients became lifetime carriers. With more than 4,000 New Yorkers developing the disease in 1907 alone, that meant that thousands of carriers like Mary Mallon were living in the city.

Opposite top: North Brother Island as seen from the air in 1937. Mary Mallon's cottage *(opposite bottom)* is circled in the overhead view.

Inside Mallon's cottage, photographed during the 1930s

How could the health department stop them all from spreading typhoid bacteria and infecting others?

William Park, who directed the laboratories, and Walter Bensel, who had overseen Mallon's capture, both spoke out about the problem. They agreed that the city had so many carriers that they couldn't possibly lock up all of them.

But Health Commissioner Thomas Darlington was proud of the drop in the typhoid fever death rate since he took office in 1904. Twenty percent fewer New Yorkers had died of typhoid despite the city's growth by half a million people over the past five years. He didn't want to release a woman known to have caused several typhoid outbreaks.

AN OFFER OF FREEDOM

The health department doctors again explained to Mallon that they wanted to help her return to her previous life. But first they had to eliminate the typhoid bacteria from her body.

The best way—maybe the only way—was to take out her gallbladder, where typhoid germs were living and dividing. They promised to get "the best surgeon in town to do the cutting."

Mallon refused. "No knife will be put on me. I've nothing the matter with my gall bladder."

The head nurse tried to persuade her. "Would it not be better for you to have it done than remain here?"

Mallon said no, it would not. She wondered if they were trying to commit murder by slicing into her: "I'm a little afraid of the people & I have a good right."

By January, ten months after Mallon was taken from the Bownes' house, doctors had failed to cure her. The health department tried another strategy. One of the Riverside Hospital doctors asked her: If she were allowed to leave the Island, where would she go?

Mallon didn't hesitate. "To N.Y.," she replied.

That wasn't the answer the New York City Department of Health wanted to hear.

Later, the head nurse brought up the subject with Mallon. The city might let her go if she said the right thing. She should write to Commissioner Darlington, the nurse suggested. Tell him that if he released her, she'd leave New York, change her name, and go live he did not. I took the Chloroform for about 3 months all told during the whole year if I should have Continued it would Certainly have Killed me for it was very Severe Every one Knows who is acquainted in any Kind of medicine that its used for Kidney trouble? When in January they were about to discharge me when the resident Phisician came to me + asked me where was I going when I got out of here naturally I said to N. Y— as there was a stop put to my getting out of here then the Supervising nurse told me I was a hopeless case + if I'd write to Dr Darlington + tell him I'd go to my Sister in Connecticut. now I have no Sister in that state or any other in the U. S.

he have the best Surgeon in town to do the Cutting, I said no no Knife will be put on me I see nothing the matter with my gall blauder Dr Wilson asked me the very same question I also told him no then he replied it might not do you any good also the Supervising nurse asked me to have an operation performed I also told her no + she made the remark would it not be better for you to have it done then remain here I told her no There is a visiting Doctor who came here in October he did take quite an interest in me he really thought I liked it here that I did not care for my freedom he asked me if I'd take some medicine if he brought it to me I said I would so he brought me some Anti-Autotox + some pills then Dr Wilson had also...

Two pages from Mary Mallon's handwritten letter detailing her suffering while detained by the health department. The 1909 letter was included in documents submitted by her lawyer to the New York State Supreme Court.

with her sister in Connecticut.

Mallon replied that she couldn't do that for one simple reason: "I have no Sister in that state or any other in the U.S."

MARY FIGHTS BACK

By July 1908, Mary Mallon had been imprisoned for more than a year. She had adopted a small fox terrier as a companion, and her boyfriend, Brichof, was allowed to visit. Still, her life on the Island was boring and dismal. For many years, she had been used to working. Now she had nothing to keep her busy.

The health department wouldn't let her go. They said it was because she was giving off typhoid bacteria. Well, Mallon didn't believe it. She had never believed it, and she was determined to prove them wrong.

Briehof agreed to help. For the next nine months,

he took samples of her feces and urine to Manhattan for tests at a private laboratory.

Every report from Ferguson Laboratories came back the same: "This specimen shows no indication of Typhoid Fever." One report said that her urine and feces were negative; however, her blood suggested that "a condition of Typhoid existed at some previous time but not at present. There will be no danger of communicating the ddisease [*sic*] to another throught [*sic*] the medium of cooking."

That was the proof Mallon wanted. The health department had no right or reason to keep her locked up.

Her resentment grew when she learned that the health department's William Park had written an article about her. In September 1908, it was published in the *Journal of the American Medical Association*.

Park wrote that Mary (he didn't give her last name) couldn't be released because she had infected more than two dozen people. During a discussion of the article at a medical conference, Dr. Milton Rosenau, director of the U.S. Public Health Service Hygienic Laboratory, referred to her as "typhoid Mary."

Mallon was livid: "I wonder how . . . Dr. Wm. H. Park would like to be insulted and put in the Journal & call him or his wife Typhoid William Park."

BREAKING NEWS

For almost two years, Mary Mallon stood alone against New York City and its health department. In the spring of 1909, an Irish attorney named George Francis O'Neill came to her rescue.

O'Neill was in his early thirties and had been practicing law in New York for about two years. No one knows how she arranged to hire him. Some say that

Mary Mallon, as depicted in the June 20, 1909, edition of the *New York American*

William Randolph Hearst, the powerful newspaper publisher, paid O'Neill's legal fees, perhaps to get her story.

However it happened, reporters at Hearst's *New York American* newspaper found out Mary's last name and the details of her capture and imprisonment. On Sunday, June 20, 1909, the paper's 800,000 readers found out, too.

A blaring headline stretched across two pages in the magazine section: "'TYPHOID MARY' MOST HARMLESS AND YET THE MOST DANGEROUS WOMAN IN AMERICA." Below the headline was a drawing depicting a parade of her victims, including 4 laundresses, 1 parlor maid, 1 footman, 1 nurse, and 3 society women. The list was loosely based on George Soper's investigation.

In its sensational article, the newspaper identified the cook Mary Mallon as "Typhoid Mary." A drawing showed her breaking skull-like eggs into a frying pan. An interview with George Soper recounted her "Extraordinary Trail of Death and Disease."

William Park was quoted, too, reassuring the public that Mary didn't spread typhoid fever through casual contact. It was through her cooking. "It is extremely unfortunate for the woman," Park said, "but it is the plain duty of the health authorities to safeguard the public from such a menace."

Although the newspaper made Mary Mallon look like a killer, it also expressed some sympathy for her. It described her as "a prisoner on New York's quarantine island." In one photograph, she is confined to a bed in Willard Parker Hospital. In another, she is huddled against a building on North Brother Island with a blanket wrapped around her to keep warm.

Mary, the newspaper said, "has committed no crime,

YET THE MOST DANGERO

nera.   1 Gentleman Visitor.   3 Society Women.   6 of a Lawyer's Family.

has never been accused of an immoral or wicked act, and has never been a prisoner in any court, nor has she been sentenced to imprisonment by any judge."

PLEA FOR FREEDOM

These words sounded as if they could have come from a lawyer's mouth. In fact, that might have been exactly where the reporter got them. George O'Neill's tactic for freeing his client was to argue that Mallon had done nothing wrong. Yet she'd been imprisoned without a court hearing or trial.

On Monday, June 28, 1909, O'Neill filed a writ of habeas corpus (which means "you have the body") in the New York State Supreme Court. In this legal document, he asked a judge to require the superintendent at Riverside Hospital to produce Mary Mallon and explain why she was being held.

A Supreme Court justice ordered the health department to bring Mallon from North Brother Island to the Supreme Court building in Manhattan the next day. She was finally getting her day in court.

... S WOMAN IN AMERICA.

1 Footman.   1 Nurse.   1 Workwoman.   2 Daughters and Their Mother.   1 Trained Nurse.   1 Parlor Maid.   1 Negro Servant Girl.

On Tuesday morning, reporters from the New York newspapers were waiting for her at the courthouse. After the *New York American*'s article nine days before, Typhoid Mary Mallon had become famous, and her nickname stuck. News about her sold papers.

Mallon hadn't been off the Island for about two years, and she took advantage of the chance to share her outrage. "I have committed no crime," she announced to reporters, "and I am treated like an outcast—a criminal. I . . . have always been healthy."

She looked it, too. Reporters described her "as rosy as you please" and having "a clear, healthy complexion, . . . bright eyes and white teeth." It seemed remarkable to them that she could be full of deadly typhoid bacteria.

Mallon pulled out a copy of the *New York American* article with a picture of her dropping skulls onto a skillet. "It's ridiculous to say I'm dangerous," she said.

She complained that no one ever spoke to her on the Island. A nurse dropped off meals at her door three times a day and rushed away. "Why should I be banished like a leper and compelled to live in solitary confinement with

An illustration representing Typhoid Mary's victims ran across two pages of the *New York American* on June 20, 1909.

only a dog for a companion?" she asked.

To some newspaper readers, it seemed unlikely that doctors and nurses who regularly treated lethal contagious diseases would ostracize Mallon. The *New York American* had printed a photo of her sitting with other women against a building on North Brother Island, clearly not in solitary confinement.

"It was the drinking water, not me that caused the trouble," Mallon insisted. "I never had typhoid in my life."

Not everyone agreed. One reporter quoted an unidentified health department doctor: "If she should be set to work in a milk store to-morrow in three months she could accomplish as much as a hostile army."

Mary Mallon (in foreground) lies in bed while being held at Willard Parker Hospital. The image was part of the *New York American* article.

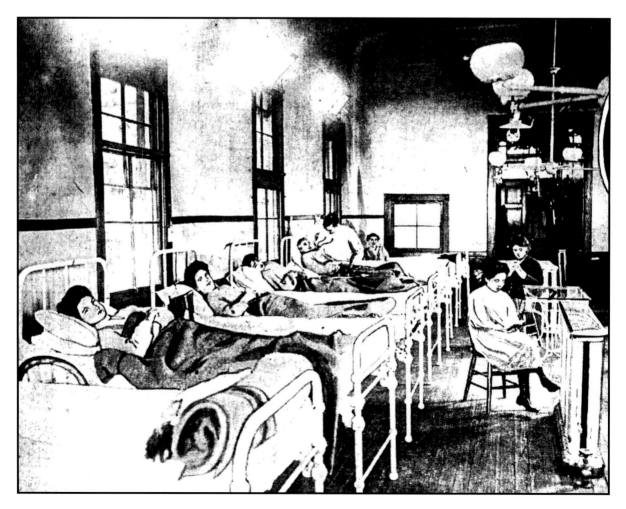

At the court hearing, the attorney representing the health department explained why Mallon was held in a contagious hospital: she is "a menace to the health of the community." The doctors were attempting to cure her infected condition, he said. She still had large amounts of bacteria in her stools, however, and should not be allowed to go free.

The attorney asked for an adjournment so that he could better prepare his case. The justice agreed, sending Mallon back to North Brother Island.

She'd been off the Island for just three hours. "I don't want to go back," she said. "It's very lonely over there."

But back she went.

THE ARGUMENTS

During the next two weeks, the lawyers on both sides argued their positions in papers submitted to the Court.

The health department's attorney provided the evidence gathered by George Soper, tracing the typhoid cases caused by Mary Mallon. A Department of Health doctor stated that "The repeated outbreaks . . . were in themselves proof that the virulence of the bacilli had remained intact."

To back up its case, the Department's attorney gave the Court twenty-eight months of its laboratory tests. From March 1907 to June 16, 1909, the lab had examined 163 of Mallon's fecal specimens and found 120 positive for typhoid bacteria. Because of the enormous amount of germs in her body and her occupation as a cook, the Department contended that she must not be released. She "would be a dangerous person and a constant menace to the public health."

The Department's attorney quoted from New York State laws, arguing that the Board of Health had the legal right to quarantine sick people. It did not need to obtain a court's permission when it was acting to prevent the spread of contagious diseases.

Mallon's lawyer, George O'Neill, asked for her release. "Mary Mallon is in perfect physical condition," he claimed. As evidence, O'Neill presented the reports from Ferguson Laboratories confirming that she was not giving off typhoid bacteria.

In the laboratory's final report on April 30, 1909, owner George Ferguson wrote: "I would state that none of the specimens submitted by you, of urine and feces, have shown Typhoid colonies." This, said O'Neill, proved that Mary Mallon "is not in any way or any degree a menace to the community."

The attorneys had made their arguments, and the case was in the hands of the justice. Until he made his decision, Mallon could do nothing but wait in her cottage facing the East River and wonder: would she ever be set free?

INTO THIN AIR

"It would be well if cooks could be selected only after careful assurance concerning their histories and personal habits." —George Soper

Mary Mallon waited two weeks to learn her fate.

On July 16, 1909, Justice Mitchell Erlanger announced his decision: "ORDERED that the said writ of Habeas Corpus be . . . dismissed and that the said petitioner, Mary Mallen [*sic*], . . . hereby is remanded to the custody of the Board of Health of the City of New York."

They weren't going to let her go.

Justice Erlanger explained that he understood Mallon's desire to be freed, but he had to side with the health department: "While the court deeply sympathizes with this unfortunate woman, it must protect the community against a recurrence of spreading the disease."

He added that if, at a future time, Mallon could prove that she had been cured, she could apply for her freedom again.

The health department had convinced Erlanger that Mallon already infected innocent people and was capable

This portrait of Mallon appeared in the *New York American* on June 30, 1909. Two drawings show her spreading deadly germs and being forced into the ambulance.

of infecting more. The evidence was her feces, which were still full of typhoid bacteria. Erlanger trusted the health department lab tests rather than those arranged by Mallon at Ferguson Laboratories.

George Ferguson ran a reputable and competent company. The discrepancy between the two sets of lab results could have had several explanations. The specimens that Mallon's friend Briehof delivered might have been mishandled before reaching Ferguson's lab. Maybe they were too old to show the bacteria. Possibly she had collected and sent feces and urine samples during the occasional times when her body wasn't giving off the bacteria.

Mary Mallon had no doubt about which results were correct. She had never given typhoid fever to anyone!

MARRIAGE PROPOSAL

Most New Yorkers approved of Justice Erlanger's decision, though they felt sorry for Mallon. After all, it wasn't her fault that a "curious freak of nature . . . has made of her a repository for typhoid germs." An editorial in the *New-York Daily Tribune* summed up the opinion of many: "It is unfortunate that, in order to secure the majority in their rights, hardship must sometimes be inflicted on the minority or on an individual." Mallon deserved to get "the best medical treatment in order that she may be cured of her strange affliction."

One man didn't seem to mind that she was "a living culture of typhoid fever bacilli." The day after the court decision, a twenty-eight-year-old farmer from Michigan named Reuben Gray wrote to Health Commissioner Thomas Darlington. He'd read about Mary Mallon's case, and he wanted to help her by offering her a home.

His farm was large and away from town, he wrote, so she wouldn't be a danger to others. Mary sounded like a good cook, the most important quality in a wife, he believed. "One thing she must know before she comes," Reuben added, "and that is that I have been insane, but it was over three years ago."

When the residents of the man's town heard about his offer, they protested that they didn't want Typhoid Mary anywhere near them. They had no reason to worry. Commissioner Darlington did not grant Reuben his wish. Mary Mallon would stay on North Brother Island.

LASHING OUT

Justice Erlanger's refusal to release Mallon increased her anger toward the Board of Health and the people who had captured and imprisoned her. Mallon lashed out at them in an interview with the *World* newspaper. "I'm persecuted!" she cried. "All the water in the ocean wouldn't clear me from this charge in the eyes of the Health Department." Mallon insisted that she had "been flung into prison without a fair trial," and even murderers were entitled to that.

She claimed that on North Brother Island she took care of the doctors' children and helped to nurse sick patients. Children loved her and always had. Doctors and nurses visited her and ate meals that she cooked. "Does that look as if I carried death with me everywhere I went?" she asked.

Yet just a few weeks before, Mallon had declared

that she was ostracized on the Island and treated like a leper. Some *World* readers found her new claims hard to believe. It didn't make sense that medically trained people would take the risk of eating food she'd prepared after they regularly found her feces teeming with typhoid bacteria.

Mallon vowed to get justice. "Will I submit quietly to staying here a prisoner all my life? No!" she told the reporter. "I will be either cleared or die where I now am."

She sent hostile letters to those she blamed for her imprisonment. One recipient was Josephine Baker, who was now director of the health department's Division of Child Hygiene. Baker was unnerved by Mary Mallon's letter and later said, "She had threatened to kill me if she could get out."

Hermann Biggs, who authorized Mallon's capture, received numerous "violently threatening letters" that distressed his family and friends. Once, during a visit to North Brother Island on health department business, Biggs happened to walk past her cottage. Mallon stood in the doorway with a whip, scowling at him. His friends were worried enough to surround him protectively, until they realized she was using the whip to train her dog.

THOUSANDS OF CARRIERS

Even though Mary Mallon had lost her bid for freedom, her case forced officials throughout the country to consider how they should handle other typhoid carriers. In 1909, at least 400,000 people in the United States suffered from typhoid fever. Thousands who recovered became carriers. It was impossible to identify them all.

Charles Chapin, health superintendent in Providence, Rhode Island, believed the country contained "a very respectable army of unrecognized sources of typhoid

Opposite: A 1909 postcard claims that lime juice kills typhoid germs. Terrified of the disease, people were willing to try anything to prevent it.

infection." Isolating the few carriers that officials could find, like Mary Mallon, was "practically useless, and therefore unjust." Instead, he recommended that carriers should not be allowed to serve food.

Milton Rosenau of the Public Health Service agreed. He said that it wasn't "necessary to imprison the bacillus carrier; it is sufficient to restrict the activities of such an individual."

Meanwhile, some doctors in the New York City Department of Health doubted they would ever be able to cure Mary Mallon. Nothing they'd tried had worked. Stronger drugs that might kill the bacteria would kill her, too. She repeatedly refused to have her gallbladder removed, and there was no guarantee that the surgery would work, anyway.

A CHANGE OF HEART

In January 1910, a new health commissioner was appointed. Dr. Ernst Lederle accepted the fact that there were likely "other persons quite as dangerous" as Mary Mallon in the city. It didn't seem fair to single her out. Lederle was willing to give Mallon a chance at freedom. "She has, in my opinion, been hounded long enough for something that is no fault of her own," he said. "I am going to do all I can to help her."

In February, the Board of Health offered Mallon a deal. It would release her if she promised not to work as a cook or handle food intended for other people. She also had to report to the health department regularly to update her whereabouts and be tested for typhoid bacteria.

Lederle announced to the New York press that Mary Mallon "has been shut up long enough to learn the precautions that she ought to take. . . . I have little fear that

Milton Rosenau (1869–1946) served as director of the U.S. Public Health Service's Hygienic Laboratory. Later he helped establish schools of public health at Harvard and the University of North Carolina at Chapel Hill.

she will be a danger to her neighbors." The doctors and nurses at North Brother Island had emphasized to her that she must wash her hands after using the toilet so that her fingers didn't spread her typhoid-laden excrement.

After being a prisoner for nearly three years, Mallon agreed to the conditions. She didn't believe that she was infected with typhoid bacteria, but she wasn't going to turn down her freedom.

Mary Mallon quietly slipped back into the city. Lederle and the health department never announced exactly when she left the Island or where she went.

SEEKING REVENGE

She was off the Island, but Mallon's life wasn't easy. Cooking had been her profession, and now she was forbidden to do it. The health department found her work as a laundress, though the wages were much less than she had made as a cook. For someone with her talents and experience, such low-skilled work was hard to accept.

The publicity during her court hearing had made her name and face infamous. Who would want to hire "Typhoid Mary" now? The city had ruined her chances of making a decent living, and Mallon wanted officials to pay for the difficulties she was having.

Her attorney, George O'Neill, came to her aid again. In December 1911, he sued the City of New York and the Department of Health on Mallon's behalf for illegally confining her. He demanded that she be paid $50,000 in damages. Mallon claimed in the legal papers that she was not now and never had been a typhoid-germ carrier.

The lawsuit held responsible several people from the health department: Darlington (the commissioner when she was captured), Lederle (the commissioner who let her go), Park (the head of laboratories), and Dr. Fred Westmoreland (the resident physician of Riverside Hospital). It also named George Soper, whom Mallon blamed for the beginning of her troubles.

O'Neill told the press, "If the Board of Health is going to send every cook to jail who happens to come under their designation of 'germ carrier,' it won't be long before we have no cooks left."

The lawsuit went nowhere, and a year later, O'Neill advised his client to drop the case. Perhaps he realized the courts would once again support the Board of Health instead of Mallon.

A SHOT IN THE ARM

While the health department kept tabs on Mary Mallon, the national efforts to control typhoid fever continued. Surgeon General Rupert Blue told the U.S. Congress, "There is probably no single disease whose study is of as great importance at the present time."

Many cities were still using rivers as sewers. Buffalo, New York, dumped its raw sewage into the Niagara River, and it flowed over the famous Niagara Falls. The rate of typhoid fever was alarmingly high in the city of Niagara Falls, New York, which took its drinking water from the river.

New York City fought its own typhoid epidemic during the summer of 1911 when 700 people became ill. Typhoid-infected sewage from a town north of the city polluted the water flowing into one of New York City's reservoirs. Later that year, the city built a filtration plant to protect the reservoir.

In 1908, Jersey City, New Jersey, became the first American city to treat its water with bacteria-killing chlorine. Others soon followed. Whenever a community introduced

chlorinated water, its typhoid rates plummeted.

The U.S. Public Health Service encouraged the nation's cities and towns to abandon outhouses and to build well-designed sewer systems. It also recommended that all milk be pasteurized to kill typhoid bacteria.

In 1910, the Service advised local officials to investigate outbreaks, trace them back to their source, and test possible carriers. The Service warned that carriers should be banned from handling food consumed by others. It advocated giving local health departments the legal power

Laundresses use large tubs, a wringer, and a drying rack to wash clothes in 1905. Mary Mallon earned much less as a laundress than as a cook.

might be exposed because of an epidemic, travel, or a profession such as nursing.

OUTBREAK!

For a while after her February 1910 release, Mary Mallon upheld her end of the agreement with the Board of Health. She checked in as she was required and submitted feces for lab tests. The bacteria hadn't gone away, and she was reminded not to cook for others.

Then sometime in 1913 or 1914, Mallon stopped showing up. No one knew where she was or what had happened to her. The mystery worried health officials.

In January 1915, the Department of Health received a report of a typhoid fever outbreak at Sloane Hospital for Women, a maternity hospital. Of the 281 patients and employees, 25 became ill, including doctors, nurses, other workers, and a patient. A nurse and a chambermaid died.

The Department knew that this hospital was meticulous about hygiene, so investigators focused on food as the outbreak's source. They uncovered an important clue when they learned that one of the sickened doctors had eaten only a single meal at the hospital. Everyone who developed typhoid had eaten that meal, too. Investigators traced the source of the bacteria to a pudding.

Coincidentally, the health department had given typhoid vaccines to some of the doctors and nurses during the previous three years. Almost as many of them became sick as those who hadn't been vaccinated. The vaccine apparently didn't protect against a large dose of food-borne bacteria.

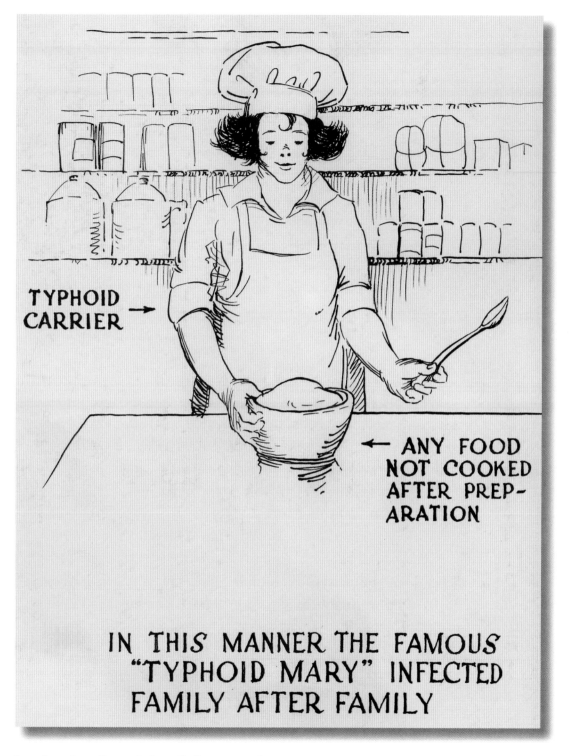

A cartoon from the early twentieth century shows how typhoid bacteria spread through uncooked food from a carrier like Typhoid Mary.

THE MISSING COOK

Investigators zeroed in on the kitchen, sampling the staff's blood. The Widal blood test of the cook who had prepared the pudding was slightly positive. But because the test wasn't always reliable, they couldn't be certain that she was the source of the outbreak.

Something else made the health inspectors suspicious. After they took the cook's blood sample, she suddenly quit her job.

Hospital officials described her as an Irish woman named Mrs. Brown, who had been working there since October 1914. Her co-workers said that when the outbreak started, they had nicknamed her "Typhoid Mary." It was all in fun. None of them had reason to suspect the cook of causing the epidemic.

The health department made it a priority to find Mrs. Brown. Over the next few weeks, investigators interviewed her acquaintances, trying to learn more about her and where she might be.

What they discovered was disturbing. The woman they sought was none other than forty-five-year-old Mary Mallon.

Someone tipped them off that she might be living in a house in another part of New York City, the Corona section of Queens. The health department put a man on lookout at the house.

On Friday, March 26, 1915, the temperature in New York hovered around the upper 30s. An occasional light rain made it a dreary day to be outside. But the officer watching the Queens house stayed alert, and it paid off.

He spotted a woman walking down the sidewalk

toward the house, her face concealed by a veil. She opened the front door and went inside.

The officer immediately called in the sighting and kept an eye on the house to make sure she didn't leave. Soon several members of the health department, including sanitary inspectors and a doctor, were rushing by car to the scene.

After they all arrived, one of them rang the doorbell. No one answered. Knowing that the woman was still inside, an officer extended a ladder to a second-floor window and climbed up. When he raised the window, a bulldog and a fox terrier greeted him with threatening barks.

He tossed meat to the dogs, and they let the health inspectors crawl inside.

As the men searched for the woman, they heard doors shutting. Someone was definitely in the house. Finally, they came to a closed bathroom door. One of the inspectors pushed it open. A middle-aged woman was huddled in a corner.

It was Mary Mallon. They had her again.

ISLAND EXILE

"It probably means exile for life."
—S. S. Goldwater

Eight years before, Mary Mallon fought like a lion when Josephine Baker cornered her at the Park Avenue brownstone. Now she gave up without a struggle. She climbed into the car with the health department doctor, and by the end of that day, she was back on North Brother Island.

This time, Mary had no lawyer to help her. George O'Neill had died of tuberculosis three months earlier. Her boyfriend, Briehof, was gone, too, dead of heart disease. Mary Mallon was alone.

Four days later, on March 30, 1915, the New York City Board of Health "approved the indefinite detention of 'Typhoid Mary' until such time as she should be declared no longer a public menace."

"It probably means exile for life," said Health Commissioner Sigismund S. Goldwater, who had taken over the position in February 1914. The health department had trusted Mallon to stop spreading her typhoid bacteria. She intentionally broke her promise, and now two people were dead.

In Josephine Baker's view, that was why the health department had to take her into custody again. "Mary . . . couldn't be trusted . . . It was her own bad behavior that inevitably led to her doom."

George Soper agreed with the Board of Health's decision. "She was known wilfully and deliberately to have taken desperate chances with human life," he wrote. Mary was once considered an "innocent victim of an infected condition," but no longer. "She was a dangerous character and must be treated accordingly."

A WITCH!

The sympathy that people once felt toward Mallon evaporated. The *New York Tribune* said that she had been given her freedom and "she deliberately elected to throw it away." One newspaper columnist declared: "The result of Typhoid Mary's excursion was disastrous. . . . There was evidently nothing to do but to shut her up and keep her out of mischief."

To many, Mary Mallon was a despicable source of germs and death. New York's *Sun* said of her: "Mary's presence in a community means serious illness, perhaps death." There was no excuse for her behavior: "This woman and other typhoid carriers . . . distribute [the germs] with their hands because they are filthy . . . they do not wash them when ordinary decency demands it."

Newspapers all across the United States reacted to Mallon's recapture. In Washington State, the *Tacoma Times* called her a "twentieth century witch" who "scatters GERMS—typhoid germs!"

Sigismund S. Goldwater (1873–1942) served as New York City health commissioner for one year before returning to his work as a hospital administrator.

UNSOLVED MYSTERY

Why had Mallon gone back to cooking? Maybe she didn't see the harm in it, because she never believed that she caused the typhoid outbreaks. Perhaps she couldn't support herself with lower-paying jobs. Or she might have been tired of the Department of Health's control over her.

The Department tried to find out where she'd been hiding. Investigators uncovered evidence that she used the aliases Marie Breshof and Mrs. Brown to get work as a cook. They didn't learn much else. The newspapers reported that she worked throughout the New York City area in hotels, restaurants, private homes, a sanatorium, and a rooming house. These stories were never proved.

Only Mary knew where she had been during those five years, and she never told.

Altogether, she was definitely linked to 49 typhoid cases and 3 deaths. Soper produced evidence that she caused 24 typhoid cases, including 1 death, from 1900 to 1907. In several of his writings, he said that there had been 2 more cases, although he gave no proof or details of them.

The outbreak at the Sloane Hospital for Women in 1915 involved 25 cases, including 2 deaths.

The health department wasn't certain how many other people Mallon might have infected. No one knew where she'd worked before George Soper picked up her trail. He hadn't been able to track everywhere she'd cooked between 1897 and 1907. Some reports claimed that while she was free from 1910 to 1915, she infected at least 6 people, but that was never verified.

It is likely that Mary Mallon triggered typhoid outbreaks that nobody ever connected to her, but probably not as many as some people claimed. According to rumors, she was behind the epidemic of 1,350 cases in Ithaca, New York, in 1903, which George Soper had investigated. That wasn't true.

Mallon's past would remain a mystery. Her future, however, was determined the day she walked out of the bathroom of the house in Queens and into the health department car. Mary Mallon would live the rest of her life on North Brother Island.

After Mallon was sent back to her North Brother Island cottage, the only part of New York she could see from her island prison was the skyline. This photograph was taken in 1907.

After returning to her tiny cottage in March 1915, she settled back into her routine on the Island. She had no choice. Mallon adopted another dog to keep her company. She cooked for herself, sewed, and read magazines, newspapers, and books. Her favorites were the novels by Charles Dickens.

The doctors continued to test her feces for typhoid bacteria, and the results came back positive most of the time. Mallon never believed it.

People on the Island learned to tread lightly with her. "She knew how to throw herself into a state of almost pathological anger," the superintendent of Riverside Hospital later said. For several years she was like a "moody, caged jungle cat."

THE CARRIER LIST

Newspaper stories about Typhoid Mary had made New Yorkers anxious. If someone who looked perfectly healthy could spread death, were they safe in hospitals, in restaurants, and even in their own homes?

After Mallon's recapture, Commissioner Goldwater reassured the public that the Department of Health was watching for typhoid carriers. Food handlers had to submit a feces sample for laboratory tests before the city allowed them to work. The Department investigated all outbreaks and monitored people after they recovered from a typhoid bout.

Everyone who was shedding typhoid bacteria had to report regularly for tests. These people were banned from jobs where they might infect others. If carriers were careful about personal hygiene, Goldwater explained, they wouldn't spread the bacteria.

George Soper offered an extra piece of advice for

carriers. "They must try to give up the senseless habit of shaking hands." He told a reporter, "The germs do not fly through the air; they are transmitted by the hands."

The Department of Health maintained a list of typhoid carriers, and it grew longer each year. In 1908, the list contained 5 names, including Mallon's. By 1915, when she returned to North Brother Island, the Department was keeping its eye on 23 people. In 1918, the number had increased to 70. Officials used a map of the city to show where each carrier lived, in case an outbreak occurred in the neighborhood.

The health department didn't always isolate a carrier in a hospital the way it had when Mallon was first captured. If officials were satisfied that the person was practicing proper hygiene and staying away from food-handling jobs, he or she was allowed to go free.

Carriers who did not cooperate were held in city hospitals, including Riverside on North Brother Island. The stay was usually temporary. The health department let a carrier go once the bacteria had disappeared from his or her body or when officials trusted the person to follow the rules.

Mary Mallon never received the same treatment, even though she likely sickened fewer people than several other carriers did (see sidebar, page 130). It was her bad luck to have been America's first healthy typhoid carrier.

When George Soper found her in 1907, officials hadn't figured out what to do with a carrier. In 1915, when they sent her back to the Island, it might have been to set an example to other carriers who considered disobeying the rules. And after all the publicity about her, nervous New Yorkers would probably have protested if she had been freed. Officials—and the public—couldn't trust a woman who refused to believe that she spread deadly bacteria.

ON THE WAY DOWN

At the end of World War I, in 1918, typhoid fever was still a major cause of death—fifth among infectious diseases, behind tuberculosis, pneumonia, infant diarrhea, and diphtheria. But the rates of infection and death were rapidly going down.

In New York City in 1919, just 854 cases were reported to the Department of Health, almost 400 fewer than the year before. Of those, 121 people died. The Department's investigations revealed that the majority of cases were from direct contact with a typhoid patient or through food contaminated by a carrier. Few were due to polluted water or milk. The efforts to clean up drinking water, improve sewage disposal, and pasteurize milk had made the difference.

Between 1900 and 1920, the number of Americans who developed typhoid fever dropped from about 400,000 to 35,000. Deaths decreased from 35,000 to fewer than 7,000. The doctors, scientists, and engineers involved in public health finally had reason to be optimistic about controlling the lethal disease.

A NEW LIFE

In 1918, after three years back on the Island, Mary Mallon's life took a turn for the better. New York State began to financially support carriers banned from food handling. Mallon was given a job as a helper in the Riverside Hospital. She liked earning money again.

A few years later, a young female doctor trained her to be an assistant in the hospital's laboratory, performing simple tests and preparing slides. Mallon became interested enough in the work to read about laboratory

Opposite: **The typhoid vaccine helped to lower infection rates. This U.S. Army researcher works on the vaccine in 1917.**

techniques in books that she found at the hospital.

Also in 1918, officials decided to let Mallon take day trips off the Island. Crossing the East River on the ferry, she visited people she knew in New York City, including old friends from before her capture. She never again tried to run away from the health department.

Eventually, Mallon accepted that the Island would be her home forever. She formed friendships with nurses, doctors, and other workers on the Island. The priests from St. Luke's Roman Catholic Church in the Bronx across the river visited her.

They all knew never to mention typhoid fever or ask Mallon about her past. She remained bitter about the way she had been treated by the health department, the city, and the public.

Mallon never allowed doctors to operate on her gallbladder. It turned out to be the right decision. The health department later studied five carriers whose gallbladders were removed. In 1921, it announced that none of the surgeries had successfully eliminated the typhoid bacteria.

As the years passed, Mallon put on weight and her vision declined until she needed eyeglasses. Soon after she turned sixty, her beloved dog died. She buried him on the island, and his absence made her life lonelier.

One December day in 1932, Mallon didn't show up as usual at the hospital lab. A concerned co-worker walked to Mallon's cottage to check on her. Mary lay on the floor, partially paralyzed. The sixty-three-year-old woman had had a stroke.

Mary Mallon would never walk again nor return to her cottage overlooking the East River. For the next six years, she was a patient at Riverside Hospital, bound to

When she was in her early sixties, Mary Mallon posed in her laboratory coat.

Mallon spent the rest of her life on the grounds of Riverside Hospital. The East River and city skyline are in the background.

a wheelchair or bed and dependent on the care of the medical staff. She suffered from heart and kidney disease, and her health steadily declined.

MERCY

November 11, 1938, was a bright, clear day and unusually warm for late fall in New York City. At 11 a.m., four Boy Scout buglers blew taps in Times Square. All traffic stopped. In New York and across the country, Americans paused for two minutes of silence to remember the end of the devastating world war exactly twenty years before.

For the first time, the United States marked Armistice Day as a legal holiday. Government offices, schools, banks, and many businesses closed. Throughout the day, parades and religious services honored the soldiers who had fought and given their lives for the nation.

On North Brother Island in the East River, Mary Mallon died of pneumonia at age sixty-nine.

The next morning, a priest conducted her funeral at St. Luke's. Fewer than a dozen friends and their families attended, including a nurse, the doctor who trained her to work in the hospital's laboratory, and a friend Mallon had known since her days of freedom.

Mallon had saved much of the money she earned at Riverside Hospital. In her will, she gave a total of about $4,000 to those friends who stood by her at the end, to the Catholic Charities organization, and to a priest who often visited her. She also left money to pay for her burial in St. Raymond's Cemetery in the Bronx. Typhoid Mary was put to rest under a gravestone that read "Jesus Mercy."

Mary Mallon had been held on North Brother Island for more than twenty-six years. She shed typhoid bacteria in her feces until the end of her life. By all accounts, she

never believed that she had given anyone typhoid fever.

Josephine Baker described her as "a pitiful creature who never committed a crime and yet who caused more deaths than the most desperate of killers." She added, "I learned to like her and to respect her point of view."

After Mallon's death, George Soper summed up the tragedy of her life: "The world was not very kind to Mary."

Typhoid Mary, 70, Disease Carrier
Mary Mallon, Immune Herself, Spread Illness Wherever She Went

Mary Wasn't the Only One

No one knows how many people Mary Mallon infected before the health department confined her. She probably wasn't the most dangerous carrier.

In August 1909, a month after Mallon lost her court battle, the New York City Department of Health noticed a sudden, unusual spike in typhoid cases. Investigators discovered that victims in one area of the city had consumed milk delivered from a town in upstate New York. The Department immediately stopped shipments from the supplier.

Next, they searched for the typhoid source in that upstate community. After interviewing local doctors and milk suppliers, investigators identified the typhoid carrier as a sixty-one-year-old dairy farmer. The man remembered having typhoid fever forty-six years earlier. Tests showed that his feces continued to teem with the bacteria. Over the years, many of his family members and townspeople had developed typhoid, but the disease was so common in the area that nobody had ever tried to track down the source.

The health department believed that the farmer infected about 400 people in his town and in New York City during the 1909 outbreak. The man had no idea that he had caused so many illnesses. He stopped working around milk and died two years later from a heart condition.

In December 1910, during Mallon's five-year freedom, the New York State Department of Health learned of an outbreak of 36 typhoid cases and 2 deaths. The Department traced the source to a summer guide in the Adirondack Mountain region. The man, nicknamed "Typhoid John," was healthy, but his feces were full of typhoid bacteria.

"John" agreed to follow treatments that doctors thought might rid his body of the bacteria, and he was not locked up. Whether the treatments worked on John is lost to history.

In 1915, the year Mary Mallon returned to North Brother Island, the New York City Department of Health discovered an outbreak in Brooklyn. Ice cream sold at a sweetshop had infected 59 people. Laboratory tests showed that the owner, Frederick Moersch, was the carrier, and the Department barred him from serving food. He wasn't quarantined, perhaps because he was supporting four children and promised to work as a plumber. In 1928, investigators on the trail of a Manhattan outbreak found Moersch making ice cream again. This time, he had sickened dozens of people.

After his second offense, Moersch ended up in Riverside Hospital, where he stayed for several years and had a job as a hospital worker. The health department attributed at least 144 cases and 6 deaths to him. Unlike Mary Mallon, Moersch eventually left North Brother Island. It's unclear why the health department let him go. He died in 1947.

In another case from the 1920s, a carrier who worked in food service infected 87 people, 2 of whom died. Tony Labella was allowed to go free after he promised to stop handling food for others and to regularly report to the health department. But the thirty-four-year-old man disappeared.

In 1922, New Jersey officials traced Labella to an epidemic of 35 cases and 3 deaths. He had broken his promise and was working on farms. The New York authorities did not lock him up. Instead, the city found him a job as a construction worker.

Although men were connected to these outbreaks, about 75 percent of carriers are women. During this period, the majority of women did not work outside their homes and, therefore, did not trigger large outbreaks that caught the attention of the health department.

In 1938, the year Mary Mallon died, New York City's list of healthy typhoid carriers contained about 400 names. Some of them had disappeared. Mallon was the only one held captive.

THE REST OF THE STORY

"Typhoid fever can be prevented."
—Centers for Disease Control and Prevention

Mary Mallon despised her nickname, but that is how the world remembers her. After more than a hundred years, the name "Typhoid Mary" still describes a person who spreads disease and death yet is immune to the danger.

Typhoid Mary has become the subject of myths, novels, and plays. Rock bands and a comic book supervillain are named after her. Mary Mallon made her mark on history and culture, although few people know anything about the woman behind the name.

She is remembered for the number of victims she infected. But Mary was herself a victim of the lethal typhoid bacterium. Even though *Salmonella* Typhi didn't make her sick or kill her, it ruined her life.

THE GERM FIGHTER

George Soper wrote several articles and gave numerous interviews about how he tracked down Mary Mallon.

Typhoid fever, spread by poor sanitation, continued to be a public health problem for decades, especially in rural areas. This family receives the vaccine around 1930.

These were published during her lifetime as well as after her death.

Soper enjoyed a long career as a sanitation engineer in New York, working for the city and as a private consultant. When the New York City subway opened in 1904, Soper investigated sanitation issues, such as bacteria levels, temperatures, and air quality, in the underground trains. For several years, he led a commission that studied the sewage pollution of New York's harbor and rivers. During World War I, Soper served as a major in the U.S. Army's Sanitary Corps.

In 1923, he became the managing director of the American Society for the Control of Cancer, the predecessor of today's American Cancer Society. By that time, the number of deaths from infectious diseases was rapidly decreasing. Typhoid, tuberculosis, diphtheria, cholera, and smallpox had been brought under control by vaccines, medicines, and better sanitation. As these diseases disappeared, cancer became one of the top four causes of death in the United States.

On June 17, 1948, George Soper died on Long Island, New York, at age seventy-eight after several years of illness. His obituary noted, "Dr. Soper was perhaps best known for his discovery of the famous typhoid carrier, 'Typhoid Mary.'"

THE BABY SAVER

Josephine Baker's career was shaped by her experiences as a medical inspector in the New York City tenements. She was appalled to find that children under age five accounted for almost 40 percent of the city's deaths. Baker considered these deaths especially tragic because they were preventable.

Baker in the early 1920s

In the summer of 1908, she convinced the New York City Department of Health to establish the Division of Child Hygiene, and the commissioner made her its director. The Division was the nation's first government agency devoted exclusively to child health. It later became a model for other cities and states.

Baker's goal was to "start babies healthy and keep them so," and she set up programs to accomplish that. Nurses went into poor neighborhoods to check on newborns and give advice to their mothers. Baby health stations distributed safe, fresh milk and information on child care. The "Little Mothers' League" taught girls from the tenements how to care for their younger siblings while their mothers were out working.

Baker arranged for regular inspections of school

buildings to ensure that they had adequate toilets and good lighting. She stationed doctors and nurses in the schools to treat children for contagious diseases.

Josephine Baker managed to impress her male colleagues who initially balked at working for a woman. She maneuvered around the politicians who tried to interfere with her work. By 1914, she had built up the child health division to nearly 700 employees.

In 1918, during World War I, Baker told an audience that 12 percent of babies in the United States died each year. "It is three times safer to be a soldier in the trenches in this horrible war," she said, "than to be a baby in the cradle in the United States." She urged the country's health departments to change this situation.

Baker left the New York City Department of Health in 1923, going on to a career in lecturing and consulting. By then, the city's infant death rate was half what it had been in 1907 and the lowest of the country's ten largest cities.

Recognized internationally as an expert on children's health, Baker wrote books and magazine columns for parents as well as professional articles for doctors. She never married or had children of her own.

On February 22, 1945, Josephine Baker died of cancer in a New York hospital at age seventy-one. The *New York Times* credited her with making New York "one of the safest instead of the worst cities for babies to be born in."

THE ISLAND

By the early 1940s, tuberculosis cases had dropped in New York because of new antibiotics, control of the disease's spread, and healthier living conditions. The city no longer needed Riverside Hospital to treat its tuberculosis patients. At the end of World War II, North Brother Island instead

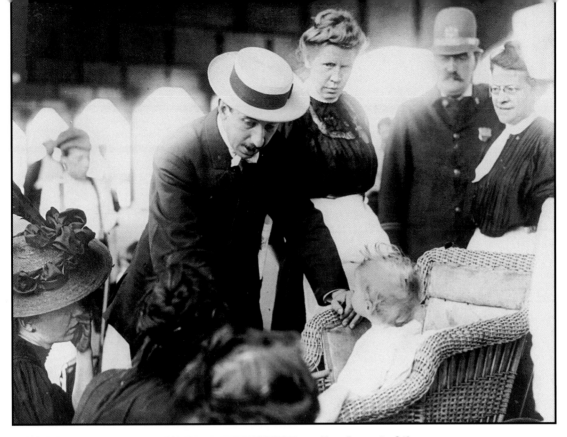

Top: As part of the New York City health department's programs to protect children, a doctor examines a baby on a hot summer day.

Bottom: Baker set up the "Little Mothers' League" to teach older girls to care for their siblings. These sisters were photographed in New York City around 1910.

Today the dock at North Brother Island has rotted and the buildings are covered with thick vegetation.

became the temporary home for a group of returning soldiers and their families.

In 1951, New York State acquired the hospital, turning Riverside into a treatment and rehabilitation center for teen drug addicts. By 1963, officials decided that the center had a poor success rate in curing addicts and cost too much to maintain. That July, the Island was abandoned.

The ferry shut down, buildings crumbled, and trees and vines took over. Flocks of birds made it their home, and the city designated the Island a bird sanctuary. Today it is closed to the public.

TYPHOID IN THE TWENTY-FIRST CENTURY

In the United States, the public health battle against typhoid fever was a success. Water filtration, chlorination, and improved sewage disposal greatly reduced the number of victims. In 1900, about 31 of every 100,000 Americans died of typhoid fever. By 1940, the rate had dropped to only 1 out of 100,000.

Today, death from typhoid is rare. The Centers for Disease Control and Prevention (CDC) estimates that about 5,700 people are infected each year. Laboratory tests confirm 300 to 400 cases. Nearly two-thirds occur in just six states with large populations: California, New York, New Jersey, Illinois, Texas, and Massachusetts.

About 80 percent of these people caught the bacteria during a trip outside the country. Most had been to India, Bangladesh, or Pakistan, where the vast majority of the world's cases occur. Parts of sub-Saharan Africa, Latin America, and south and east Asia also have high typhoid rates, particularly in urban slums.

Typhoid spreads easily where human waste contaminates drinking water and food. As many as 2.5 billion people worldwide live without basic sanitation, with a billion of them routinely defecating on open ground. Nearly 800 million have no access to clean water. In these areas, people tend to wash their hands less often and without the soap that helps remove bacteria.

International public health experts estimate that each year about 22 million people become sick with typhoid and between 200,000 and 800,000 die. But it's not a precise count. Many victims live in developing countries that don't monitor typhoid cases. In places without laboratory testing facilities, typhoid is often misdiagnosed (and miscounted) because its early symptoms resemble other diseases such as malaria.

VACCINE PROTECTION

Travelers to high-risk countries can protect themselves by being vaccinated. Most U.S. cases occur in travelers who had not received a vaccine before visiting these parts of the world.

The typhoid vaccine, first used in the early 1900s, has improved over the decades. Today, two types are licensed in the United States and used internationally, one taken by mouth and the other injected. In areas where typhoid fever is unusual (the United States, Canada, Japan, and Western Europe), the vaccines are given to travelers, families of carriers, and lab workers who might be exposed to the bacteria.

These vaccines are safe, though they aren't perfect, especially for people living in high-typhoid countries. The vaccines protect less than 70 percent of those who get one, and they can't be used on children younger than age two. Protection lasts just two to five years. Researchers are currently trying to develop better vaccines that protect a higher percentage of people for a longer time.

The existing vaccines have controlled epidemics, however. After a cyclone hit Fiji in 2010, health officials worried about a typhoid outbreak. Storm damage and flooding caused sewage to contaminate the drinking water. The islands already had one of the world's highest rates of the disease. Seventy thousand people were vaccinated, helping to avoid a potentially devastating epidemic.

THE ANTIBIOTIC WEAPON

During the lifetimes of Mary Mallon, George Soper, and Josephine Baker, careful nursing was the only treatment for typhoid. From 10 to 30 percent of patients died. For many years, doctors experimented with various drugs, but nothing worked.

Then in 1948, researchers discovered a soil bacterium from Venezuela that destroyed *Salmonella* Typhi. Chemists figured out how to make a drug based on this bacterium, and it dramatically cured typhoid victims.

Today, several different antibiotics are available. With these drugs, patients rarely suffer the kind of complications that once caused death. In areas of the world where patients receive antibiotic treatment, the death rate has dropped to about 1 percent.

But *Salmonella* Typhi has become resistant to many of the life-saving antibiotics. In numerous countries throughout the world, people can buy them without a prescription, and the drugs have been used improperly. This has led to a growing number of typhoid cases in which the antibiotics don't kill the bacteria. Without effective drugs to treat patients, health experts fear that the fatality rate will rise again.

OTHER TYPHOID MARYS

In many American communities, doctors are required by law to report typhoid fever cases to their local health department. Depending on local laws, patients may have to submit their feces and urine for testing for at least three months or until they stop shedding the bacteria. Someone who tests positive after a year is classified as a chronic carrier.

Infected people are usually allowed to go to work or school, and they're told to wash hands carefully after using the toilet. But workers in food preparation, health care, or child care typically can't return to their jobs until their tests are negative. In many places, chronic carriers are banned from these occupations. Local health departments often monitor carriers, making sure that they follow rules about personal hygiene and work.

The majority of carriers are cured after taking antibiotics for several weeks. When this treatment isn't successful, the best alternative is removal of the gallbladder, where the bacteria frequently live and multiply on gallstones. The surgery is safer and more likely to cure the carrier than it was during Mary Mallon's lifetime. But no treatment for carriers is 100 percent effective.

Health departments have extensive legal powers to protect the public from contagious diseases like typhoid. They can order testing, isolation, and treatment. The extent of a person's right to challenge the decision in court depends on the state and the disease.

OUTBREAKS CONTINUE

Typhoid outbreaks still occasionally happen in the United States. Today's epidemiologists trace typhoid infections to the source and find out how the bacteria spread. An outbreak usually starts with a healthy carrier preparing food, unaware that he or she is infecting others.

Sometimes, however, the source is someone with typhoid fever symptoms. In 2013, a worker in the café of a luxury department store in San Francisco was diagnosed with the disease. The health department investigation revealed that the person had been infected outside the United States.

To alert people who had eaten in the café, officials quickly issued a public statement with a list of typhoid symptoms. They advised anyone with symptoms to seek medical care, to avoid handling food and beverages for others, and to stop caring for young children and hospital patients.

Imported food has also caused outbreaks. In 2010, 12 people in three western states developed typhoid. Public health officials interviewed the victims and tested samples of foods they'd eaten.

The investigators traced the typhoid bacteria to shakes made from the frozen pulp of mamey, a tropical fruit. The frozen mamey came from a Guatemalan factory, where it had been contaminated. The factory hadn't properly pasteurized the pulp to kill bacteria, as required by American food regulations. Twelve years earlier, mamey from the same company caused at least 16 typhoid cases in Florida.

HOPE FOR THE FUTURE

Scientists are studying the DNA sequence of *Salmonella* Typhi's genome to find weaknesses that they can use to fight typhoid fever. Clues may lead to better diagnostic tests, antibiotics, treatments, and vaccines.

Other researchers are trying to understand how typhoid bacteria remain in a carrier's body without causing symptoms. The work is challenging because *Salmonella* Typhi doesn't cause disease in other animals, and certain experiments on humans would be unethical.

Projects in developing countries are aimed at protecting the water supply from contamination and purifying it by chlorination. Unfortunately, in many parts of the world, these sanitation improvements could take years to achieve.

Someday, research and public health efforts may succeed in eradicating typhoid fever. When that happens, *Salmonella* Typhi will no longer inflict pain and suffering on communities the way it did in Ithaca more than a hundred years ago. And no one will ever become a "Typhoid Mary" again.

Wash Those Hands

Too many Americans don't wash their hands after using the toilet. That's the conclusion of recent studies conducted in public bathrooms.

The Centers for Disease Control and Prevention (CDC) recommends washing with soap and water for twenty seconds, about the time it takes to hum the "Happy Birthday" song twice. This prevents germs from spreading from feces and urine. To keep unwanted bacteria out of your food, wash your hands again before preparing and eating it.

Find more about when and how to wash, as well as the science behind the recommendations, at cdc.gov/handwashing.*

*Website active at time of publication.

The twenty-two-year-old typhoid patient in this 1840 painting died within five days of falling ill.

FAMOUS TYPHOID VICTIMS
Famous People and Their Families Suffered, Too

1 Abigail Adams (1744–1818), First Lady and wife of the second U.S. president, John Adams (1735–1826). At age seventy-three. *Died*, just three days after her fifty-fourth wedding anniversary.

Prince Albert (1819–1861), husband of Great Britain's Queen Victoria (1819–1901). At age forty-two. *Died*. Albert and Victoria's son, the future **King Edward VII** (1841–1910). At age thirty. *Recovered*.

2 **Louisa May Alcott** (1832–1888), author of *Little Women* and other books for young readers. At about age thirty-one, while nursing soldiers during the Civil War. *Recovered.*

3 **Grover Cleveland** (1837–1908), twenty-second and twenty-fourth U.S. president. At age eighteen. *Recovered.* As mayor of Buffalo, New York, in 1882, Cleveland initiated the building of the city's first sewer system, an improvement that dramatically lowered typhoid rates.

4 **Stephen A. Douglas** (1813–1861), U.S. senator from Illinois and Democratic Party candidate who lost to

Republican Abraham Lincoln in the 1860 presidential race. At age forty-eight. *Died.*

George Ferris (1859–1896), inventor of the Ferris wheel. At age thirty-seven. *Died.*

Martha and Mary Jefferson, daughters of **Thomas Jefferson** (1743–1826), who later became the third U.S. president. At about ages sixteen and ten, while in Paris with their father in the late 1780s. *Recovered.*

5 **Andrew Johnson** (1808–1875), seventeenth U.S. president. At age fifty-six. *Recovered.* Two months later, in April 1865, President Abraham Lincoln was assassinated and Vice President Johnson became president.

Anne Carter Lee, daughter of Civil War general **Robert E. Lee** (1807–1870). Age twenty-three. *Died.* Her father received word of her death in October 1862 while he was commanding Confederate troops.

6 Tad and Willie Lincoln, sons of the sixteenth U.S. president, **Abraham Lincoln** (1809–1865). Tad (on right) at age eight. *Recovered.* Willie at age eleven. *Died.* Both boys became ill in early 1862. Of all the children of U.S. presidents, Willie was the only one to die in the White House.

Katherine McKinley, daughter of **William McKinley** (1843–1901), who later became the twenty-fifth U.S. president. At age three in 1875. *Died.* Her death left the McKinleys forever childless.

7 Cecile and Jeanne Pasteur, daughters of French bacteriologist **Louis Pasteur** (1822–1895). Jeanne at age nine in 1859. *Died.* Cecile at age twelve in 1866. *Died.*

8 **Franklin D. Roosevelt** (1882–1945), thirty-second U.S. president. At age thirty, during his successful 1912 run for New York State Senate. *Recovered.*

9 Mittie Roosevelt, mother of **Theodore Roosevelt** (1858–1919), who later became the twenty-sixth U.S. president. At age forty-eight on Valentine's Day 1884. *Died.* On the same day, Roosevelt's first wife, Alice, also died, after giving birth to their daughter.

Franz Schubert (1797–1828), Austrian composer. At age thirty-one. *Died.*

10 **William Howard Taft** (1857–1930), twenty-seventh U.S. president. At about age ten. *Recovered.*

11 Olivia Clemens, wife of author Samuel Clemens, who was known as **Mark Twain** (1835–1910). At age twenty-six in 1871. *Recovered.*

12 **Orville and Wilbur Wright**, inventors and builders of the first successful airplane. Orville (on right, 1871–1948), at age twenty-five. *Recovered.* Wilbur (1867–1912), at age forty-five. *Died.*

GLOSSARY

Antibiotic: a drug used to destroy disease-causing bacteria.

Antibody: a protein produced by the body in response to the presence of an antigen (a substance normally foreign to the body) to which the antibody binds.

Bacilli: rod-shaped bacteria.

Bacteria: microscopic one-celled organisms.

Bacteriologist: a scientist who studies bacteria.

Bile: a yellow-green fluid produced by the liver that helps digest fat in food.

Bile ducts: tubes that carry bile from the liver and gallbladder.

Cholera: an infectious and sometimes fatal disease with symptoms of extreme diarrhea and dehydration, caused by a bacterium.

Contagious disease: an illness spread by contact with a person who has the disease.

Culture: to grow bacteria in a special nutrient-containing gel or liquid in order to identify and study them; the colony of bacteria that grows this way.

Diphtheria: a contagious and sometimes fatal upper-respiratory disease caused by a bacterium.

Dysentery: an intestinal disease with symptoms of severe diarrhea and abdominal pain.

Epidemiologist: a scientist who studies where diseases originate, how they spread, and how they can be controlled.

Excrement: body waste; usually refers to feces.

Feces: body waste discharged from the intestines.

Gallbladder: the small organ that stores bile until it's needed for food digestion.

Germ theory: the idea that diseases can be caused by microorganisms.

Grippe: another name for influenza.

Infectious disease: an illness caused by an organism such as a bacterium, virus, or parasite that invades the body.

Malaria: an infectious disease with symptoms of fever and chills caused by parasitic microbes transmitted by mosquitoes.

Microbiologist: a scientist who studies microorganisms.

Microorganism (or **microbe**): a microscopic organism, such as a bacterium or virus.

Pasteurization: a process of killing disease-causing microbes by heating.

Quarantine: forced isolation or restriction to prevent the spread of a contagious disease.

***Salmonella* Typhi**: bacterium that causes typhoid fever.

Smallpox: an often fatal contagious disease caused by a virus. Symptoms include high fever and skin sores.

Tuberculosis: a serious and sometimes fatal lung disease caused by a bacterium.

Typhoid fever: an infectious disease caused by a bacterium that spreads through food and water contaminated with body waste.

Typhus: an infectious disease caused by a bacterium that is transmitted by fleas, lice, mites, and ticks.

Urine: liquid body waste discharged from the kidneys.

Vaccine: a special preparation of killed or weakened microbes that triggers the body to produce immunity to a disease.

Timeline

1869	*September 23*—Mary Mallon is born in Cookstown, County Tyrone, Ireland.
1870–1910	More than 20 million immigrants come to the United States.
1870	*February 3*—George A. Soper is born in Brooklyn, New York.
1873	*November 15*—S. Josephine Baker is born in Poughkeepsie, New York.
1880	Karl Eberth identifies the typhoid bacterium.
1883	Mallon immigrates to America.
1896	Georges Widal develops a test for typhoid fever.
1898	Spanish-American War.
1900	*September*—TYPHOID: Mamaroneck, New York, family; 1 victim.
	September 8—A deadly hurricane strikes Galveston, Texas; Soper helps with cleanup.
1901	*December*—TYPHOID: New York City family; 1 victim.
1902	*June*—TYPHOID: Drayton family, Dark Harbor, Maine; 9 victims.
	November—Robert Koch announces the discovery of healthy typhoid fever carriers.
1903	*January*—TYPHOID: Epidemic begins in Ithaca, New York; the city water supply is blamed.
	March–August—Soper helps control the Ithaca epidemic.
1904	*June*—TYPHOID: Gilsey family, Sands Point, New York; 4 victims.
1906	*August–September*—TYPHOID: Warren family, Oyster Bay, New York; 6 victims.
	October—TYPHOID: Kessler family, Tuxedo Park, New York; 1 victim.
	Fall—Soper is hired to investigate the Oyster Bay outbreak and begins his search for Mallon.
1907	*February*—TYPHOID: Bowne family, New York City; 2 victims, including 1 death.
	March—Soper tells New York City Department of Health about Mallon. She is captured and detained.
1908	*Summer*—Baker becomes director of the Division of Child Hygiene.
	September—The nickname "typhoid Mary" first appears in print, in the *Journal of the American Medical Association*.

1909	*June 20*—Popular press first uses nickname "Typhoid Mary," in the *New York American*.
	June 28—Mallon's lawyer files a petition for her release in New York State Supreme Court.
	June 29—Mallon appears in court.
	July 16—Court orders Mallon returned to North Brother Island.
1910	*February*—Mallon is released by the health commissioner.
1911	U.S. Army requires all soldiers to receive the typhoid vaccine.
	December—Mallon files a lawsuit against New York City.
1914	*July*—World War I breaks out.
	October—Mallon is hired as a cook at Sloane Hospital for Women in New York City.
1915	*January–February*—TYPHOID: Sloane Hospital for Women; 25 victims, including 2 deaths.
	March 26—Mallon is arrested and taken back to North Brother Island.
1917–18	United States fights in World War I until its end.
1918	Mallon is hired as a helper at Riverside Hospital and allowed day trips off North Brother Island.
1923	Soper becomes managing director of the American Society for the Control of Cancer. Baker retires from the Department of Health and begins a speaking and consulting career.
1932	*December*—Mallon suffers a debilitating stroke.
1938	*November 11*—Mary Mallon dies on North Brother Island. Veterans (Armistice) Day is observed for the first time in the United States.
1945	*February 22*—S. Josephine Baker dies in New York City.
1948	Scientists discover an antibiotic to treat typhoid fever.
	June 17—George Soper dies on Long Island, New York.
1963	North Brother Island is abandoned.

FOR MORE INFORMATION*

ON THE TYPHOID MARY CASE
NONFICTION

Typhoid Mary: Captive to the Public's Health by Judith Walzer Leavitt. Boston: Beacon Press, 1996.

    This is the most thorough and well-researched book on Mary Mallon and her detention on North Brother Island.

"Typhoid Mary: The Most Dangerous Woman in America" (DVD). Nancy Porter Productions and WGBH Educational Foundation, 2004. Also available on YouTube. youtube.com/watch?v=Mc8O9EnAuLo

    The *Nova* episode is based on Leavitt's book and discusses the case using interviews and dramatizations.

The Most Dangerous Woman in America (website). PBS and WGBH Educational Foundation. pbs.org/wgbh/nova/typhoid

    The online companion to the *Nova* episode provides a program transcript, teacher's guide, and links to information about the history of quarantines and the work of epidemiologists. Play the role of an epidemiologist in the interactive game Disease Detective. Read the transcript of Mallon's 1909 letter.

"The Curious Career of Typhoid Mary" by George A. Soper. *Bulletin of the New York Academy of Medicine*, October 1939. Available at the website of the U.S. National Library of Medicine. ncbi.nlm.nih.gov/pmc/articles/PMC1911442

*Websites active at time of publication

Read Soper's 1939 account of how he tracked down Mary Mallon, the last of several published articles that he wrote about the case.

Fighting for Life by S. Josephine Baker. New York: New York Review of Books, 2013.

This paperback edition of Baker's 1939 autobiography includes her account of the Mallon case.

"The Most Horrible Seaside Vacation." Radiolab. radiolab.org/story/169882-typhoid-mary

Listen to a conversation about the Typhoid Mary case, including interviews with historians and a visit to abandoned North Brother Island.

"How to Get to North Brother Island." Radiolab. radiolab.org/story/170476-how-get-north-brother-island

See recent photos of the Island's overgrown landscape and destroyed buildings.

"True Story Behind Typhoid Mary." *Dark Matters*, Science Channel. sciencechannel.com/tv-shows/dark-matters-twisted-but-true/videos/true-story-behind-typhoid-mary.htm

Watch a short video clip that dramatizes Soper's search for Mary Mallon.

FICTION

Fever by Mary Beth Keane. New York: Scribner, 2013.

The adult novel re-creates the life of Mary Mallon. Keane meshes known facts with her imagination to fill in the many gaps in the historical record.

Deadly by Julie Chibbaro. New York: Atheneum Books for Young Readers, 2011.

The young adult novel tells the story of a teen girl working as a lab assistant during the Typhoid Mary period. As fiction, the story strays considerably from the historical facts about major players and events.

ON TYPHOID FEVER

"Typhoid Fever."
Centers for Disease Control and Prevention.
cdc.gov/nczved/divisions/dfbmd/diseases/typhoid_fever

The CDC site includes useful information, both general and technical. Find out where typhoid rates are high and the ways to avoid being infected when traveling. Read about the available vaccines and drugs used to treat the disease.

"Typhoid Fever."
World Health Organization.
who.int/topics/typhoid_fever/en

This site provides links to information about vaccines, recent international outbreaks, and the conditions that allow typhoid to spread.

Author's Note

My training in biology and my interest in history make me curious about illnesses that were once common in the United States but are rare today. Who brought these diseases under control, and how did they do it?

While researching pellagra for my book *Red Madness: How a Medical Mystery Changed What We Eat*, I read about several typhoid fever outbreaks of the early 1900s. Public health officials were then battling both diseases. In 1903, my hometown of Ithaca, New York, suffered through a typhoid epidemic. Around the same time, the "Typhoid Mary" outbreaks occurred in New York City. When I realized that one man, George Soper, played a key role in both events, I was hooked on the typhoid story.

My goal in writing this book was to tell the story as accurately as possible. All direct quotations come from primary sources and are cited in the Source Notes. My descriptions of historical incidents and conversations are based on first-person accounts and on published interviews with the participants.

To find out what was known about typhoid fever in the early twentieth century, I read medical books and journals from that period. For twenty-first-century information, I interviewed medical experts and reviewed recent journal articles and books.

To learn about Ithaca's typhoid outbreak in 1903, I turned to local newspaper articles, interviews, and reports of the scientific investigations from that period; George Soper's book about his cleanup work; and scrapbooks kept by Cornell students throughout the epidemic. The Cornell University Library maintains an enlightening collection of letters and telegrams about the outbreak sent to and from the university's president. Daily updates from the student infirmary document the spread of the disease. A secondary source, the 2011 book *The Epidemic: A Collision of Power, Privilege, and Public Health* by David DeKok, examines the politics and business dealings that surrounded the Ithaca outbreak.

I also relied on my personal knowledge of the city, university, and geography. My house is less than two miles from the probable source of the outbreak—Six Mile Creek.

Tracking down the truth about Mary Mallon was challenging. She never wrote an autobiography, and scant information exists about her life before her capture. Mallon was reluctant to discuss her status as a typhoid carrier or her experiences as a cook. She gave only two confirmed interviews with the press. One six-page letter, written in her own hand, provides insight into her thoughts and feelings during the early years of her quarantine.

In addition to Mallon's letter and interviews, I gathered material from other primary sources, including court documents; S. Josephine Baker's newspaper interviews and autobiography, *Fighting for Life*; and Soper's newspaper and journal articles about his investigation.

Several people discussed their encounters with Mary Mallon in books, newspapers, magazines, and professional journals. I was cautious about the authors' biases and faulty memories. Whenever reports of an incident differed, I stuck to the facts on which the most reliable sources agreed.

The best secondary source about Mary Mallon is Judith Walzer Leavitt's well-researched book from 1996, *Typhoid Mary: Captive to the Public's Health*. For information about the New York City Health Department in the early 1900s, I used various sources, including John Duffy's work on public health and the book *Hives of Sickness*, edited by David Rosner. Charles-Edward Amory Winslow's biography of Hermann Biggs and Baker's autobiography provided additional details about the Department during this period.

I discovered that many published versions of the Typhoid Mary story contain mistakes or are fictionalized accounts. By exploring census data, obituaries, and New York City's Social Registry, I was able to clear up some inaccuracies. One error has persisted for a hundred years: The Park Avenue home where George Soper discovered Mary Mallon was owned by Walter "Bowne," not "Bowen." The first known death attributed to Mallon—the Bownes' daughter—has often been erroneously depicted as a little girl. She was a young woman.

Many questions about the Mary Mallon case have no clear answers. Did she genuinely believe that she was healthy and free of typhoid bacteria, as she claimed? Or was she aware that she was a carrier and simply not care whom she infected? New York City health officials felt it was their duty to protect the public from typhoid fever. But did they do the right thing when they isolated Mallon on North Brother Island? Should they have handled her differently? I leave it to the reader to decide.

In 1915, George Soper observed: "We have a great many lessons to learn from this Mallon case." Today, the case still raises important issues that are worth considering. When a deadly, highly contagious, and untreatable disease strikes, what do we expect health authorities to do? What government actions would—or should—we tolerate? Does the protection of a city's population trump the rights and freedom of an individual?

The events of a century ago can guide us as we confront these questions now and in the future.

SOURCE NOTES*

The source of each quotation in this book is found below. The citation indicates the first words of the quotation and its document source. The document sources are listed either in the bibliography or below.

CHAPTER ONE (page 8)

"I am an innocent . . .": Mallon, quoted in "'Typhoid Mary' Never Ill, Begs Freedom," *New York American*, June 30, 1909.

CHAPTER TWO (page 11)

"One very disagreeable . . .": Sedgwick, p. xxxiv.

"Sanitary Engineer . . .": *The Municipal Year Book 1902*, edited by M. N. Baker. New York: Engineering News Publishing, 1902, p. iii.

"germ detective": "Justice on the Trail of the Subway Germ," *New York Times*, February 17, 1905.

"Dirt, diarrhea . . .": William T. Sedgwick, quoted in Chapin, p. 128.

"discharges from . . .": Metropolitan Sewerage Commission of New York, 1910, p. 497.

"less than one . . .": same as above.

CHAPTER THREE (page 23)

"The death . . .": "Another Student Dies," *Ithaca Daily News*, February 13, 1903.

"a scum . . .": "Ithaca's Formidable Health Problem," by J. C. Bayles, *New York Times*, March 12, 1903.

"death-dealing . . .": "Fever Scourge Spreads; Ithaca in Great Panic," *Evening World* (New York, NY), February 23, 1903.

"DO NOT . . .": Margaret Harvey, dormitory warden, Sage College, Cornell University, from the Isabel Dolbier Emerson Scrapbook, 1899–1903, Division of Rare and Manuscript Collections, Cornell University Library.

"very sick": Cornell Infirmary Daily Report, February 4, 1903, Typhoid Fever Epidemic (Ithaca, NY) Records.

*Websites active at time of publication

"Much concern . . .": "Fever Patients in City More Than Four Hundred,"
    Ithaca Daily News, February 9, 1903.

"a student of . . .": "Student Dies," *Ithaca Daily News*, February 17, 1903.

"Hoping that the . . .": letter from William R. Schoenborn to J. G.
    Schurman, February 24, 1903, Typhoid Fever Epidemic
    (Ithaca, NY) Records.

"Scourge of . . .": *New-York Tribune*, February 6, 1903.

"I cannot but . . .": letter from Arthur C. Babson to J. G. Schurman,
    February 16, 1903, Typhoid Fever Epidemic (Ithaca, NY) Records.

"Fever-Stricken . . .": *Evening World* (New York, NY), February 23, 1903.

CHAPTER FOUR (page 32)

"Typhoid is one . . .": letter from George A. Soper to Ithaca mayor
    George W. Miller, August 25, 1903, Typhoid Fever Epidemic
    (Ithaca, NY) Records.

"It was nauseating . . .": Soper, quoted in "No Typhoid in the Harbor,"
    New York Times, January 8, 1909.

"city . . . in a condition . . .": Soper, "The Epidemic of Typhoid Fever at
    Ithaca," p. 441.

"a competent, experienced . . .": "Ithaca's Formidable Health Problem,"
    by J. C. Bayles, *New York Times*, March 12, 1903.

"It is certainly . . .": Jordan, April 4, 1903, p. 915.

"the city stood . . .": "Will Spend Money to Stop Epidemic,"
    Ithaca Daily News, March 5, 1903.

"Dr. Soper is . . .": "Dr. Soper, State Expert Explains Precautions Ithaca
    Is Now Taking," *Ithaca Daily News*, March 16, 1903.

"Among such a . . .": Soper, "The Epidemic of Typhoid Fever at
    Ithaca," pp. 451-52.

"His death is . . .": "Student Fever Victim," *Ithaca Daily News*,
    March 14, 1903.

"We are dealing . . .": Soper, "Full Report Made on the Epidemic,"
    Ithaca Daily News, May 8, 1903.

"millions of . . .": same as above.

"Do you think . . .": letter from Harry E. Carver to J. G. Schurman,
    March 27, 1903, Typhoid Fever Epidemic (Ithaca, NY) Records.

"pleasing, generous . . ." and "bright light . . .": "Victim of Typhoid,"
    Ithaca Daily News, May 6, 1903.

"eliminate 97 . . ." and "the water will be . . .": Soper, quoted in
    "Penalty for Drinking Filtered Water," *New-York Tribune*,
    August 30, 1903.

"When I took my bath . . .": "Penalty for Drinking Filtered Water,"
    New-York Tribune, August 30, 1903.

"all sanitarians . . .": letter from Commissioner Daniel Lewis to
    Dr. Edward Hitchcock, March 24, 1903, Typhoid Fever Epidemic
    (Ithaca, NY) Records.

"the sole stay . . .": J. G. Schurman, *Report to the Board of Trustees of
    Cornell University*, April 19, 1903, Typhoid Fever Epidemic
    (Ithaca, NY) Records.

"Seldom has . . .": Soper, "The Epidemic of Typhoid Fever at
    Ithaca," p. 449.

CHAPTER FIVE (page 44)

"All the skill . . .": Sedgwick, p. xxv.

"an epidemic fighter": Soper, "The Curious Career of Typhoid Mary,"
    p. 700.

"The most important . . .": Soper, "The Work of a Chronic Typhoid Germ
    Distributor," p. 2019.

"Servants who . . .": Soper, "Typhoid Mary," p. 5.

CHAPTER SIX (page 53)

"We have here . . .": Soper, "The Work of a Chronic Typhoid Germ
    Distributor," p. 2022.

"a beautiful . . .": Soper, quoted in "'Typhoid Mary' Has Reappeared,"
    New York Times, April 4, 1915.

"Under suitable . . .": Soper, "The Curious Career of Typhoid Mary,"
    p. 704.

"I had to say . . .": same as above.

"I thought I could . . .": Soper, "Typhoid Mary," p. 7.

"I wanted specimens . . .": Soper, "The Curious Career of Typhoid Mary,"
    p. 704.

"If she would answer . . .": same as above.

"I felt rather . . .": same as above.

"meant her . . .": same as above, p. 705.

"prostrated . . .": Soper, quoted in "'Typhoid Mary' Has Reappeared,"
    New York Times, April 4, 1915.

"menace . . .": Soper, "The Curious Career of Typhoid Mary," p. 705.

"the specific . . .": Reed, p. 202.

CHAPTER SEVEN (page 64)

"She came out . . .": Baker, p. 75.

"Disease is . . .": "Public Health Is Purchasable," by Hermann Biggs, in
    *Monthly Bulletin of the Department of Health of the City of
    New York*, October 1911, p. 226.

"both sides . . ." and "that the world . . .": Baker, p. 27.

"at all costs . . .": same as above, p. 28.

"the one thing . . .": same as above, p. 29.

"her husband . . .": same as above, p. 49.

"It reeked . . .": same as above, p. 56.

"The whole . . .": same as above, p. 57.

"I climbed . . ." and "There was no . . .": same as above, p. 58.

"that something could . . .": same as above, p. 59.

"mass of . . .": same as above, p. 60.

"a clean . . .": same as above, p. 73.

"No.": Mallon, quoted in Baker, p. 73.

"if Mary . . .": Baker, p. 74.

"this seemingly . . .": Baker, p. 73.

"I expect you . . .": Walter Bensel, quoted in Baker, p. 74.

"For another . . .": Baker, p. 75.

"like being . . .": same as above.

CHAPTER EIGHT (page 78)

"She is practically . . .": "Bellevue Prisoner Typhoid Magazine,"
    New York American, April 2, 1907.

"a human . . .": William H. Park, quoted in "Woman 'Typhoid Factory'
    Held as a Prisoner," *Evening World* (New York, NY), April 1, 1907.

"rosy-cheeked": "Woman 'Typhoid Factory' Held as a Prisoner," *Evening
    World* (New York, NY), April 1, 1907.

163

"living fever . . .": Walter Bensel, quoted in same as above.

"The Lord . . .": same as above.

"I have been . . .": letter by Mary Mallon, undated, filed with *In the Matter of the Application for a Writ. . . .*

"a human vehicle . . .": "Bellevue Prisoner Typhoid Magazine," *New York American*, April 2, 1907.

"This woman . . .": Walter Bensel, quoted in same as above.

"prominent . . .": "Bellevue Prisoner Typhoid Magazine," same as above.

"Her language . . .": "Woman 'Typhoid Factory' Held as a Prisoner," *Evening World* (New York, NY), April 1, 1907.

"Many people . . .": Soper, "The Curious Career of Typhoid Mary," p. 707.

"You don't keep . . .": same as above.

"You don't need . . .": same as above.

"There is very . . .": Baker, p. 77.

"forcible . . .": Winslow, *The Life of Hermann M. Biggs*, p. 187.

CHAPTER NINE (page 88)

"The Most Dangerous . . .": "'Typhoid Mary,' Most Harmless and Yet the Most Dangerous Woman in America," *New York American*, June 20, 1909.

"No knife . . .": letter by Mary Mallon, undated, filed with *In the Matter of the Application for a Writ. . . .*

"nervous . . .": same as above.

"If I should . . .": same as above.

"thanks to . . .": same as above.

"the best surgeon . . .": same as above.

"Would it not . . .": same as above.

"I'm a little . . .": same as above.

"To N.Y.": same as above.

"I have no . . .": same as above.

"This specimen . . .": letter by George A. Ferguson, April 23, 1909, filed with *In the Matter of the Application for a Writ. . . .*

"a condition . . .": letter by George A. Ferguson, September 2, 1908, filed with same as above.

"typhoid Mary.": Milton Rosenau, quoted in Park, p. 982.

"I wonder how . . .": letter by Mary Mallon, filed with *In the Matter of the Application for a Writ. . . .*

"Extraordinary . . .": *New York American*, June 20, 1909.

"It is extremely . . .": William H. Park, quoted in same as above.

"a prisoner . . .": *New York American*, same as above.

"has committed . . .": same as above.

"I have committed . . .": Mallon, quoted in "'Typhoid Mary' Never Ill, Begs Freedom," *New York American*, June 30, 1909.

"as rosy . . .": "'Typhoid Mary' in Court," *Sun* (New York, NY), June 30, 1909.

"clear, healthy . . .": "'Typhoid Mary' Never Ill, Begs Freedom," *New York American*, June 30, 1909.

"It's ridiculous . . .": Mallon, quoted in "'Typhoid Mary' Asks Her Freedom," *New-York Tribune*, June 30, 1909.

"Why should I . . .": Mallon, quoted in "'Typhoid Mary' Never Ill, Begs Freedom," *New York American*, June 30, 1909.

"It was the drinking . . ." and "I never had . . .": same as above.

"If she should . . .": "'Typhoid Mary' in Court," *Sun* (New York, NY), June 30, 1909.

"a menace . . .": "'Typhoid Mary' Asks Her Freedom," *New-York Tribune*, June 30, 1909.

"I don't want . . .": Mallon, quoted in same as above.

"The repeated . . .": statement by Fred S. Westmoreland, July 1, 1909, filed with *In the Matter of the Application for a Writ. . . .*

"would be . . .": same as above.

"Mary Mallon . . .": brief by George Francis O'Neill, July 10, 1909, filed with same as above.

"I would state . . .": letter from George A. Ferguson to Mary Mallon, April 30, 1909, filed with same as above.

"is not in any . . .": brief by George Francis O'Neill, July 10, 1909, filed with same as above.

CHAPTER TEN (page 103)

"It would be well . . .": Soper, quoted in "The Biological Society of Washington," *Science*, New Series, May 31, 1907, p. 865.

"ORDERED . . .": order by Mitchell Erlanger, filed with *In the Matter of the Application for a Writ. . . .*

"While the court . . .": Mitchell Erlanger, quoted in "'Typhoid Mary' Must Stay," *New York Times*, July 17, 1909.

"curious freak . . .": "Not a Case for Levity," *New-York Daily Tribune*,
    July 26, 1909.

"It is unfortunate . . .": same as above.

"the best . . .": same as above.

"a living culture . . .": "He'd Marry 'Typhoid Mary,'" *Sun* (New York, NY),
    July 21, 1909.

"One thing she . . .": Reuben Gray, quoted in same as above.

"I'm persecuted!" and "All the water . . ." Mallon, quoted in "'I'm
    Persecuted!' Is Plaintive Plea of 'Typhoid Mary,'" *World* (New York,
    NY), July 20, 1909.

"been flung into prison . . .": "'I'm Persecuted!' Is Plaintive Plea of
    'Typhoid Mary,'" *World* (New York, NY), July 20, 1909.

"Does that look . . .": Mallon, quoted in same as above.

"Will I submit . . .": same as above.

"I will be either . . .": same as above.

"She had threatened . . .": Baker, p. 76.

"violently . . .": Winslow, *The Life of Hermann M. Biggs*, p. 199.

"a very respectable . . .": Chapin, p. 138.

"practically useless . . .": same as above, p. 110.

"necessary to . . .": Milton Rosenau, quoted in "The Biological
    Society of Washington," *Science*, New Series, May 31, 1907, p. 864.

"other persons . . .": Ernst Lederle, quoted in "'Typhoid Mary' Freed,"
    New York Times, February 21, 1910.

"She has . . .": Ernst Lederle, quoted in "'Typhoid Mary' Is Free;
    Wants Work," *New York American*, February 21, 1910.

"I am going to do . . .": Ernst Lederle, quoted in "'Typhoid Mary' Freed,"
    New York Times, February 21, 1910.

"has been shut up . . .": same as above.

"If the Board . . .": George Francis O'Neill, quoted in "'Typhoid Mary'
    Asks $50,000 from City," *New York Times*, December 3, 1911.

"There is probably . . .": *Annual Report of the Surgeon General of the
    Public Health Service of the United States for the Fiscal Year 1912*,
    Washington, DC: Government Printing Office, 1913, p. 11.

"hold in quarantine . . .": "What the Local Health Officer Can Do
    in the Prevention of Typhoid Fever," by L. L. Lumsden,
    Public Health Reports, February 4, 1910, p. 118.

"reasonable . . .": same as above.

CHAPTER ELEVEN (page 118)

"It probably . . .": S. S. Goldwater, quoted in "Witch in N.Y.,"
by K. W. Payne, *Tacoma* (WA) *Times*, April 6, 1915.

"approved the indefinite . . .": "Put Car-Crowd Ban on Lexington Av.,"
New York Times, March 31, 1915.

"Mary . . . couldn't . . .": Baker, quoted in "Dr. Baker Tells How She Got
Her Woman," by Isabelle Keating, *Brooklyn Eagle*, May 8, 1932.

"It was her own . . .": Baker, p. 75.

"She was known . . ." and "innocent . . ." and "She was a dangerous . . .":
Soper, "Typhoid Mary," p. 13.

"she deliberately . . .": "'Typhoid Mary' Reappears," *New York Tribune*,
March 29, 1915.

"The result . . .": "The 'Carrier' Problem," *New York Tribune*,
August 28, 1915.

"Mary's presence . . .": "Exile for Life May Be Fate of 'Typhoid Mary,'"
Sun (New York, NY), March 28, 1915.

"This woman . . .": "Caught at Last," *Sun* (New York, NY), March 31, 1915.

"a twentieth century . . .": "Witch in N.Y.," by K. W. Payne,
Tacoma (WA) *Times*, April 6, 1915.

"She knew how . . .": John Cahill, quoted in McLaughlin, p. 470.

"moody, caged . . .": Walker, p. 23.

"They must try . . .": Soper, "Typhoid Mary," p. 15.

"The germs do not . . .": Soper, quoted in "'Typhoid Mary' Has
Reappeared," *New York Times*, April 4, 1915.

"a pitiful creature . . .": Baker, quoted in "Dr. Baker Tells How She Got
Her Woman," by Isabelle Keating, *Brooklyn Eagle*, May 8, 1932.

"I learned to like . . .": Baker, p. 76.

"The world . . .": Soper, "The Curious Career of Typhoid Mary," p. 709.

CHAPTER TWELVE (page 133)

"Typhoid fever . . .": "Typhoid Fever," Centers for Disease Control and
Prevention, cdc.gov/nczved/divisions/dfbmd/diseases/typhoid_fever.

"Dr. Soper . . .": "Dr. G. A. Soper Dies; Fought Epidemics,"
New York Times, June 18, 1948.

"start babies . . .": Baker, p. 108.

"It is three times . . .": Baker, quoted in "Open Drive to Save 4,700 Babies Here," *New York Times*, May 17, 1918.

"one of the safest . . .": "Dr. Baker Is Dead; Health Expert, 71," *New York Times*, February 23, 1945.

AUTHOR'S NOTE (page 157)

"We have . . .": Soper, quoted in "'Typhoid Mary' Has Reappeared," *New York Times*, April 4, 1915.

BIBLIOGRAPHY

Baker, S. Josephine. *Fighting for Life*. New York: New York Review of
    Books, 2013.

Blake, Nelson Manfred. *Water for the Cities: A History of the Urban
    Water Supply Problem in the United States*. Syracuse, NY:
    Syracuse University Press, 1956.

Bollet, Alfred Jay. *Plagues & Poxes: The Impact of Human History
    on Epidemic Disease*. New York: Demos Medical Publishing, 2004.

Bourdain, Anthony. *Typhoid Mary: An Urban Historical*. New York:
    Bloomsbury Publishing, 2001.

Chapin, Charles V. *The Sources and Modes of Infection*. New York:
    John Wiley and Sons, 1910.

Crump, John A., Stephen P. Luby, and Eric D. Mintz. "The Global
    Burden of Typhoid Fever." *Bulletin of the World Health Organization*,
    May 2004: 346–53.

Crump, John A., and Eric D. Mintz. "Global Trends in Typhoid and
    Paratyphoid Fever." *Clinical Infectious Diseases*,
    January 15, 2010: 241–46.

Cutler, David, and Grant Miller. "The Role of Public Health
    Improvements in Health Advances: The Twentieth Century
    United States." *Demography*, February 2005: 1–22.

DeKok, David. *The Epidemic: A Collision of Power, Privilege, and
    Public Health*. Guilford, CT: Lyons Press, 2011.

Dolfman, Michael L., and Denis M. McSweeney. *100 Years of U.S.
    Consumer Spending: Data for the Nation, New York City, and Boston*.
    Washington, DC: Bureau of Labor Statistics, 2006.

Dowling, Harry F. *Fighting Infection: Conquests of the Twentieth
    Century*. Cambridge, MA: Harvard University Press, 1977.

Duffy, John. *A History of Public Health in New York City, 1866–1966*.
    New York: Russell Sage Foundation, 1974.

———. *The Sanitarians: A History of American Public Health*. Urbana:
    University of Illinois Press, 1990.

Fenster, Julie M. *Mavericks, Miracles, and Medicine: The Pioneers Who
    Risked Their Lives to Bring Medicine into the Modern Age*.
    New York: Carroll and Graf, 2003.

Furman, Bess. *A Profile of the United States Public Health Service, 1798–1948*. Washington, DC: U.S. Department of Health, Education, and Welfare; National Institutes of Health; and National Library of Medicine, 1973.

Garbat, Abraham L. *Typhoid Carriers and Typhoid Immunity: Omnis Typhus Ex Typho*. New York: Rockefeller Institute for Medical Research, 1922.

Gonzalez-Escobedo, Geoffrey, Joanna M. Marshall, and John S. Gunn. "Chronic and Acute Infection of the Gall Bladder by *Salmonella* Typhi: Understanding the Carrier State." *Nature Reviews Microbiology*, January 2011: 9–14.

Grob, Gerald N. *The Deadly Truth: A History of Disease in America*. Cambridge, MA: Harvard University Press, 2002.

Hays, J. N. *Epidemics and Pandemics: Their Impacts on Human History*. Santa Barbara, CA: ABC-CLIO, 2005.

In the Matter of the Application for a Writ of Habeas Corpus for the Production of Mary Mallon. New York Supreme Court, Special Term, Part 2, (June 28–July 22) 1909. New York (NY) County Clerk Archives, File WR-M 258.

Jordan, Edwin O. "The Typhoid Epidemic at Ithaca." *Journal of the American Medical Association*, March 21, 28, and April 4, 1903.

Kammen, Carol. *Ithaca: A Brief History*. Charleston, SC: History Press, 2008.

Kraut, Alan M. *Silent Travelers: Germs, Genes, and the "Immigrant Menace."* New York: Basic Books, 1994.

Leavitt, Judith Walzer. *Typhoid Mary: Captive to the Public's Health*. Boston: Beacon Press, 1996.

———. "'Typhoid Mary' Strikes Back: Bacteriological Theory and Practice in Early Twentieth-Century Public Health." *Isis*, December 1992: 608–29.

Leavitt, Judith Walzer, and Ronald L. Numbers, eds. *Sickness and Health in America: Readings in the History of Medicine and Public Health*. 3rd ed. Madison: University of Wisconsin Press, 1997.

Loharikar, Anagha, et al. "Typhoid Fever Outbreak Associated with Frozen Mamey Pulp Imported from Guatemala to the Western United States, 2010." *Clinical Infectious Diseases*, July 1, 2012: 61–66.

Lynch, Michael F., et al. "Typhoid Fever in the United States, 1999–2006." *Journal of the American Medical Association*, August 26, 2009: 859–65.

McLaughlin, Mary C. "Mary Mallon: Alias Typhoid Mary." In *The American Irish Revival: A Decade of the Recorder, 1974–1983*, edited by Kevin M. Cahill, 461–74. Port Washington, NY: Associated Faculty Press, 1984.

Mendelsohn, J. Andrew. "'Typhoid Mary' Strikes Again: The Social and the Scientific in the Making of Modern Public Health." *Isis*, June 1995: 268–77.

Metropolitan Sewerage Commission of New York. *Present Sanitary Condition of New York Harbor and the Degree of Cleanness Which Is Necessary and Sufficient for the Water*. New York: Wynkoop Hallenbeck Crawford, 1912.

———. *Sewerage and Sewage Disposal in the Metropolitan District of New York and New Jersey*. New York: Martin B. Brown Press, 1910.

Mullan, Fitzhugh. *Plagues and Politics: The Story of the United States Public Health Service*. New York: Basic Books, 1989.

Park, William H. "Typhoid Bacilli Carriers." *Journal of the American Medical Association*, September 19, 1908: 981–82.

Reed, Walter, Victor C. Vaughan, and Edward O. Shakespeare. *Origin and Spread of Typhoid Fever in U.S. Military Camps During the Spanish War of 1898*. Vol. 1. Washington, DC: Government Printing Office, 1904.

Rosner, David, ed. *Hives of Sickness: Public Health and Epidemics in New York City*. New Brunswick, NJ: Rutgers University Press, 1995.

Roumagnac, Philippe, et al. "Evolutionary History of *Salmonella* Typhi." *Science*, November 24, 2006: 1301–04.

Sedgwick, William T. "Typhoid Fever: A Disease of Defective Civilization." Introductory essay in *Typhoid Fever: Its Causation, Transmission and Prevention* by George C. Whipple. New York: John Wiley and Sons, 1908.

Shere, Kalpana D., Marcia B. Goldberg, and Robert H. Rubin. "*Salmonella* Infections." In *Infectious Diseases*, edited by Sherwood L. Gorbach, John G. Bartlett, and Neil R. Blacklow. 2nd ed. Philadelphia: W. B. Saunders, 1998.

Slayton, Rachel B., Kashmira A. Date, and Eric D. Mintz. "Vaccination for Typhoid Fever in Sub-Saharan Africa." *Human Vaccines & Immunotherapeutics*, April 2013: 1–4.

Soper, George A. "The Curious Career of Typhoid Mary." *Bulletin of the New York Academy of Sciences*, October 1939: 698–712.

———."The Epidemic of Typhoid Fever at Ithaca, N.Y." *Journal of the New England Water Works Association*, 1904: 431–61.

———."Typhoid Mary." *The Military Surgeon*, July 1919: 1–15.

———."The Work of a Chronic Typhoid Germ Distributor." *Journal of the American Medical Association*, June 15, 1907: 2019–22.

Stevenson, Lloyd G. "Exemplary Disease: The Typhoid Pattern." *Journal of the History of Medicine*, April 1982: 159–81.

Sufrin, Mark. "The Case of the Disappearing Cook." *American Heritage*, August 1970: 37–43.

Thirty-Third Annual Report of the State Department of Health of New York for the Year Ending December 31, 1912. Albany: J. B. Lyon, 1913.

Typhoid Fever Epidemic (Ithaca, NY) Records, 1901–1906. Division of Rare and Manuscript Collections, Cornell University Library.

Walker, Stanley. "Typhoid Carrier No. 36." *The New Yorker*, January 26, 1935: 21–25.

Whipple, George C. *Typhoid Fever: Its Causation, Transmission and Prevention*. New York: John Wiley and Sons, 1908.

Wills, Christopher. *Yellow Fever, Black Goddess: The Coevolution of People and Plagues*. Reading, MA: Addison-Wesley Publishing, 1996.

Winslow, Charles-Edward Amory. *The Conquest of Epidemic Disease: A Chapter in the History of Ideas*. Princeton, NJ: Princeton University Press, 1944.

Winslow, C-E. A. *The Life of Hermann M. Biggs, M.D., D.Sc., LL.D.: Physician and Statesman of the Public Health*. Philadelphia: Lea and Febiger, 1929.

Ziporyn, Terra. *Disease in the Popular American Press: The Case of Diphtheria, Typhoid Fever, and Syphilis, 1870–1920*. New York: Greenwood Press, 1988.

The following periodicals:

American Journal of Nursing

American Journal of Public Health

British Medical Journal

Brooklyn [NY] *Eagle/Daily Eagle*

Bulletin of the World Health Organization

Clinical Infectious Diseases

Cornell Daily Sun

Cornell University Alumni News

Evening World/World [New York, NY]

Indian Journal of Medical Research

Ithaca [NY] *Daily Journal*

Ithaca [NY] *Daily News*

Journal of the American Medical Association

Journal of Global Health

Lancet

New York American

New York Daily News

New Yorker

New York Times

New York Tribune/Daily Tribune

Public Health Reports

Saturday Globe [Utica, NY]

School Health News

Science

Sun [New York, NY]

Tacoma [WA] *Times*

INDEX

PICTURE CREDITS